Beehive

Workbook

1

Jessica Finnis

OXFORD
UNIVERSITY PRESS

Starter Unit
Hello!

1 Complete the names. **Emma Tang Hector ~~May~~ Nina Omar**

1 

M a y

2 

___ m ___ ___

3 

___ ___ ___ g

4 

___ ___ c ___ ___ ___

5 

___ i ___ ___

6 

___ ___ m ___

2 Write. **Nina ~~Hello!~~ I'm your What's**

1 

2 

3 What's missing? Write.

a b c d e ___ g ___ i

___ k l ___ n o ___ q

___ ___ t u v ___ x ___ ___

4 Write the number.

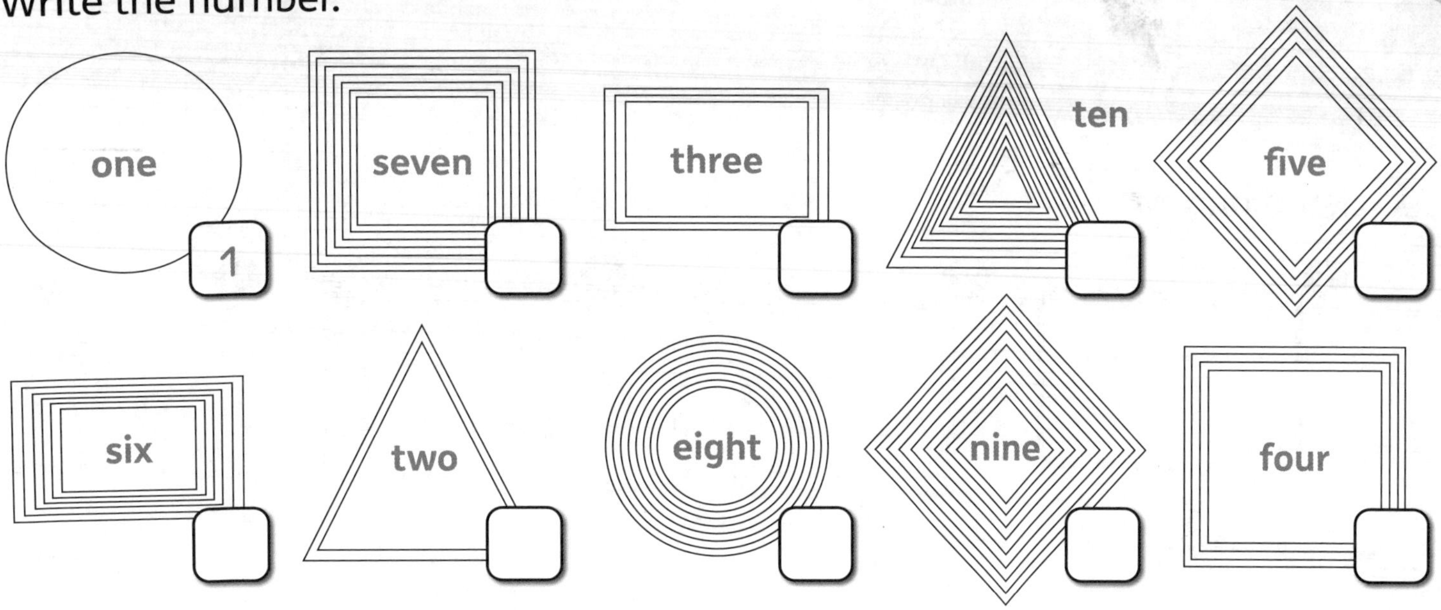

5 Write the missing numbers.

1	four	five	six
2	one	______	three
3	eight	______	ten
4	______	______	seven
5	______	two	______
6	six	______	______

6 Write.

1

How old are you?
I'm ______.

2

______ you?
I'm ______.

3

______?
______

1 At school
Lesson 1 Words

1 Read and circle.

1
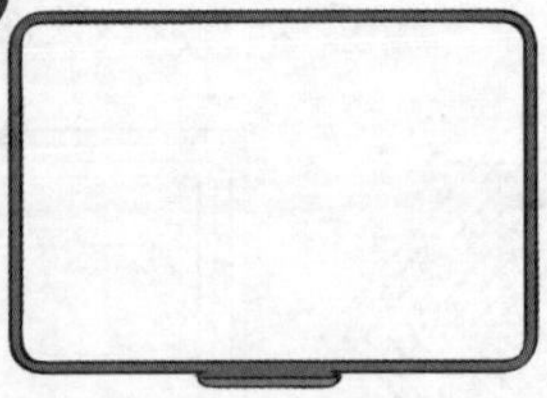
board
window

2

door
window

3
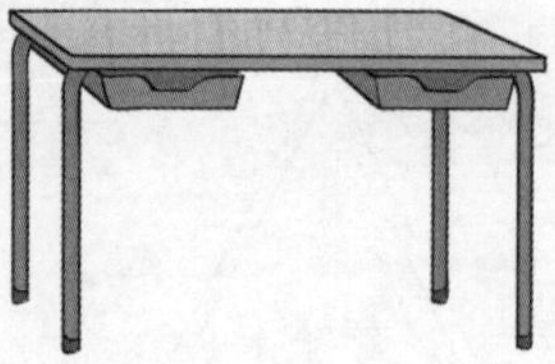
desk
chair

4

cupboard
chair

5
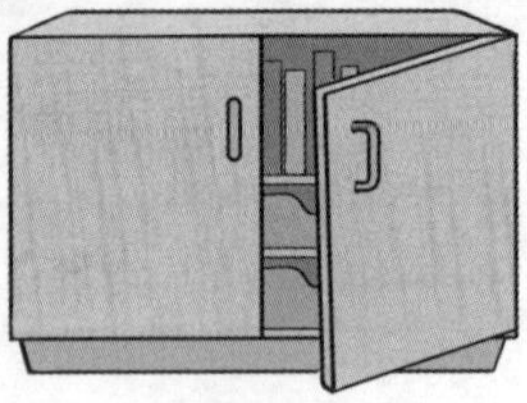
cupboard
clock

6

desk
door

7

bin
clock

8

board
bin

2 Write.

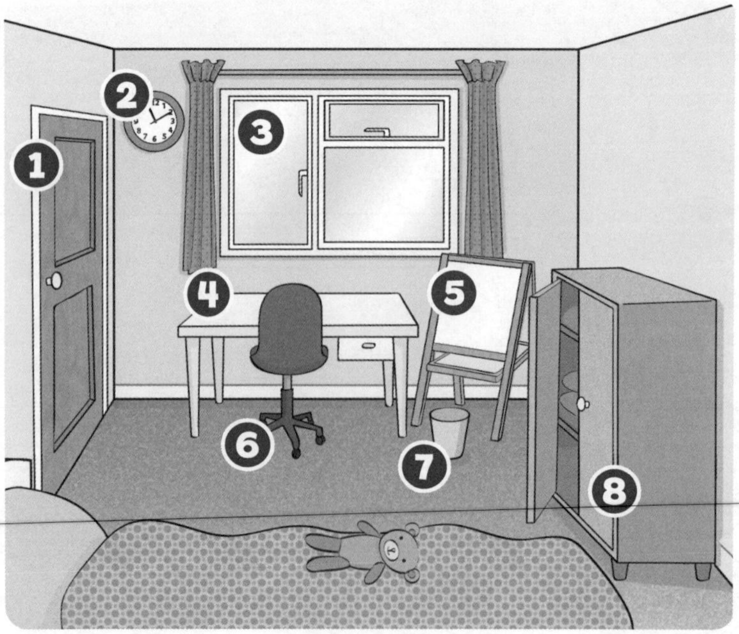

1 door

2 ____________

3 ____________

4 ____________

5 ____________

6 ____________

7 ____________

8 ____________

3 Write the letters. Then tick ✔ or cross ✘.

a	b	c	d	e	f	g	h	i	j	k	l	m
1	2	3	4	5	6	7	8	9	10	11	12	13
n	**o**	**p**	**q**	**r**	**s**	**t**	**u**	**v**	**w**	**x**	**y**	**z**
14	15	16	17	18	19	20	21	22	23	24	25	26

1 b o a r d (2 15 1 18 4)  ✘

2 ___ ___ ___ ___ ___ (3 8 1 9 18)  ☐

3 ___ ___ ___ ___ ___ (3 12 15 3 11) 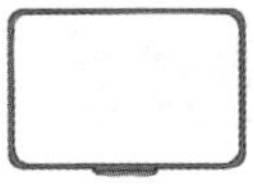 ☐

4 ___ ___ ___ ___ (4 5 19 11)  ☐

5 ___ ___ ___ (2 9 14)  ☐

6 ___ ___ ___ ___ (4 15 15 18)  ☐

4 Read and number.

a Show me the door. 3

b Show me the cupboard. ☐

c Show me the bin. ☐

d Show me the desk. ☐

e Show me the clock. ☐

f Show me the window. ☐

1 

2 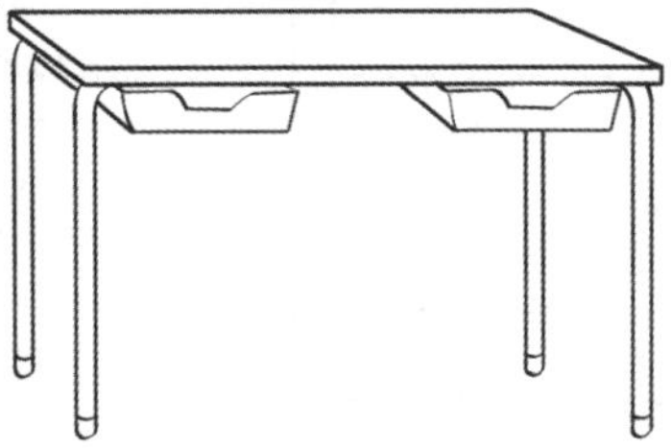

3 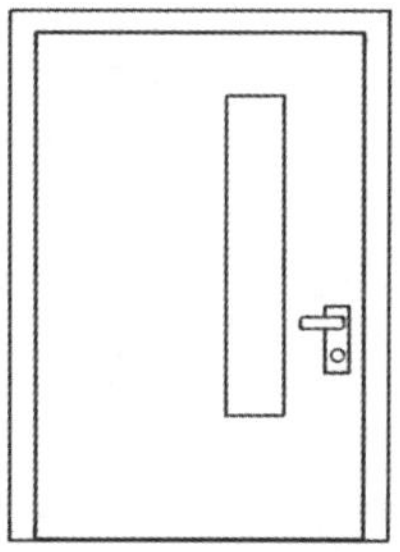

4 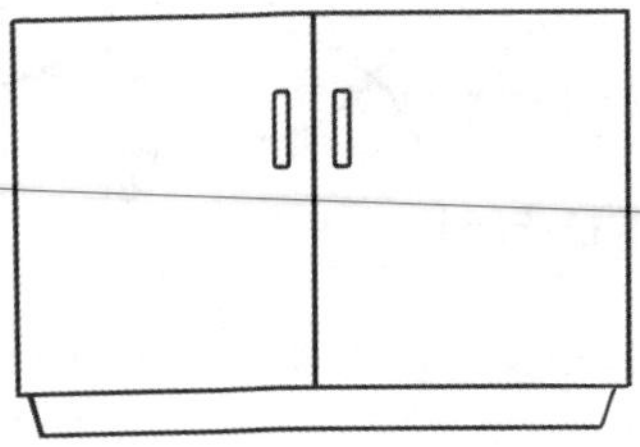

5 

6 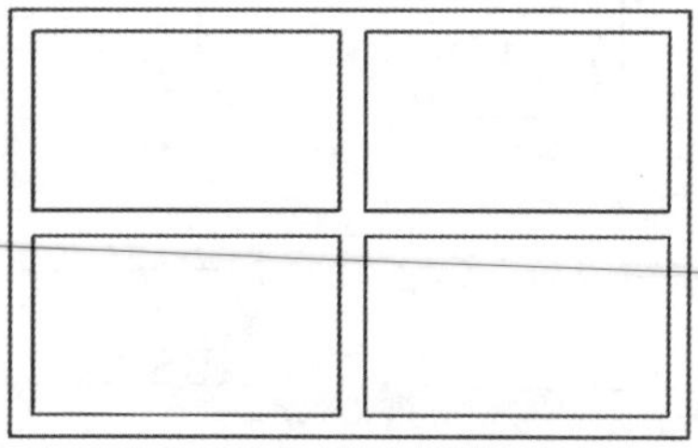

1 Order the words. Then look and write the letter.

1 board. It's a — It's a board. [e]

2 It's bin. a — ______ [ ]

3 a chair. It's — ______ [ ]

4 clock. a It's — ______ [ ]

5 desk. It's a — ______ [ ]

a

b

c

d
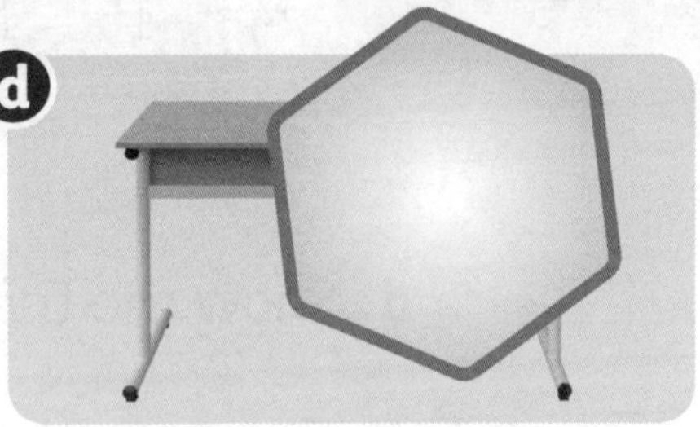

e

2 Colour and write.

1
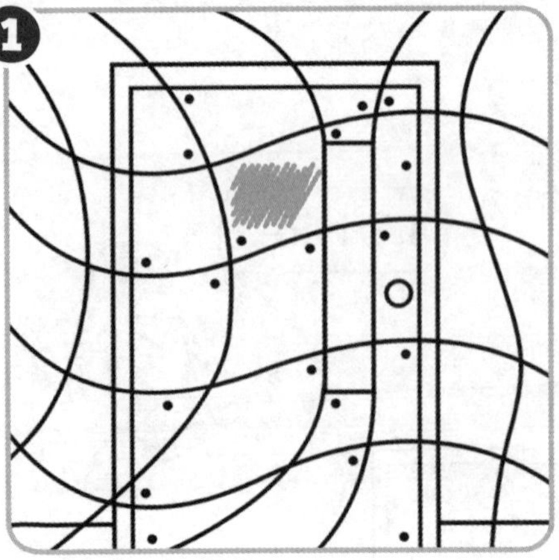

What is it?

It's a ______.

2
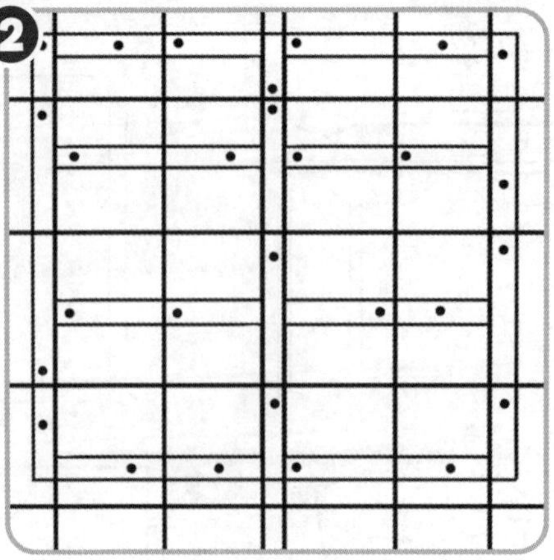

______ is it?

It's a ______.

3
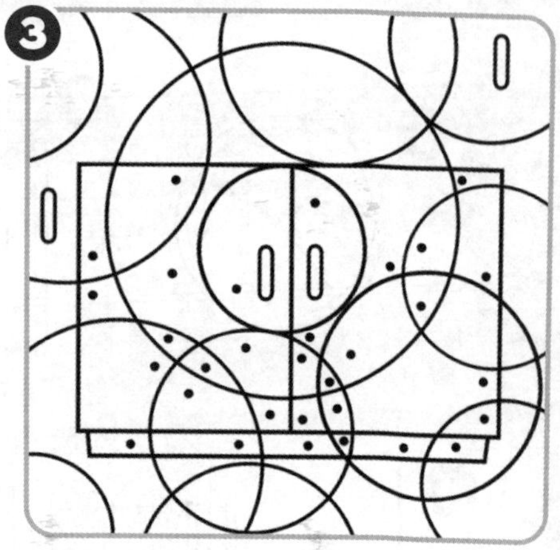

What ______?

______

3 Read and number.

What is it?

1 It's a door.

2 It's a cupboard.

3 It's a bin.

4 It's a window.

5 It's a board.

6 It's a desk.

7 It's a chair.

8 It's a clock.

4 Write.

1

What is it?
It's a chair.

2

______________________?
____

3

______________________?
____

4

______________________?
____

5

______________________?
____

6

______________________?
____

Go to Grammar check page 124

1 Read and colour.

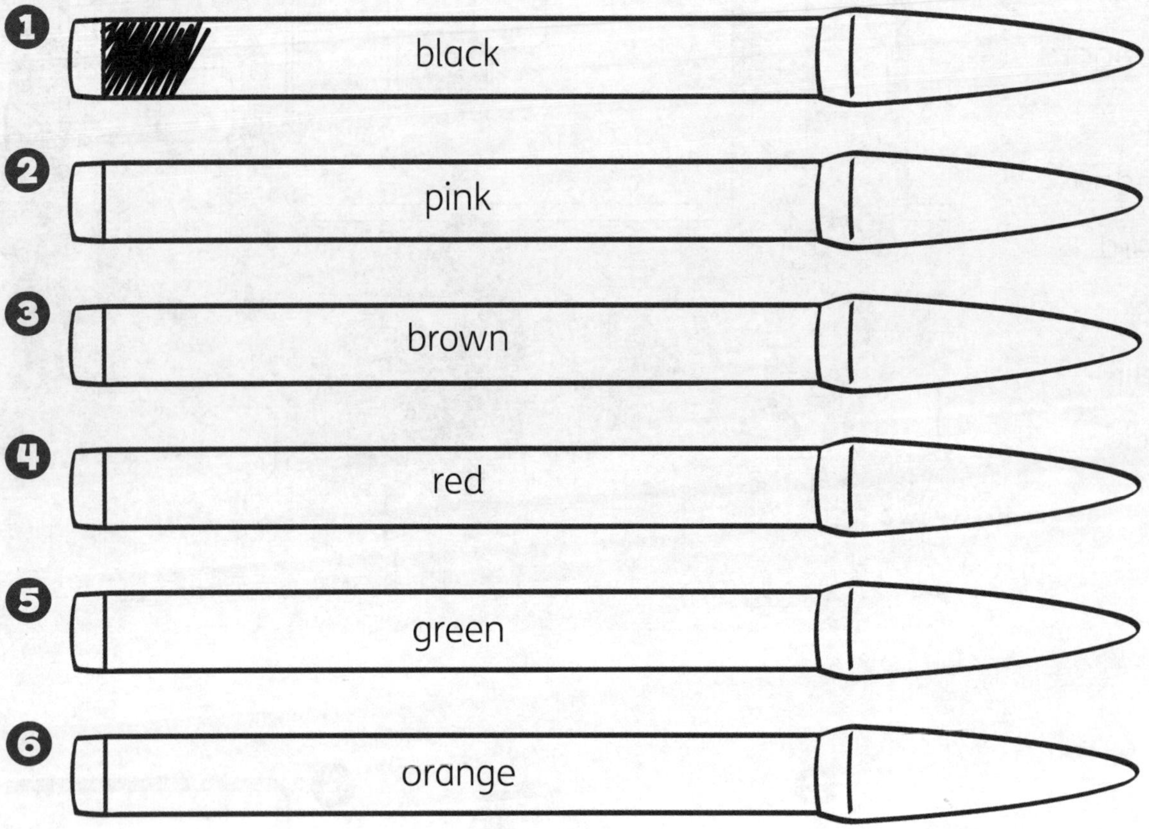

2 Choose colours. Then colour and write.

blue	**yellow**	~~**grey**~~	**purple**	**white**	**green**

Number one = grey ______________________

______________________ ______________________

______________________ ______________________

3 Write. **is it It's** **black grey white**

1

What colour is it ?

It's ____________.

2

What colour ________ ?

____

3

What colour ________ ?

____

4 Choose colours. Then colour and write.

1 What colour is the door? It's white.

2 What colour is the clock? ____________

3 ____________ is the bin? ____________

4 ____________ is the chair? ____________

5 ____________? ____________

6 ____________? ____________

➜ Go to Grammar check page 124

1 Lesson 4 Story

1 Look at the pictures. What classroom objects can you see?

2 Read the story.

Let's paint!

3 Read again and write.

1 

What colour is the desk? It's ______________.

2 

What colour is the chair? It's ______________.

3 

What colour is the cupboard? ______________ grey.

4 Write the letter.

1 This is black. ☐

2 Look, it's grey! ☐

a 

b 

5 Circle, tick ✔ and colour.

1 **Circle.**
My favourite part of the story is

1 2 3
4 5 6

2 **Tick ✔.**
My favourite character is

☐ 

☐  ☐ 

3 **Colour.**
How many stars for the story?

Reading

1 Write. **classroom** ~~**playground**~~ **student** **teacher**

1

playground

2

3

4

2 Look, read and number.

My school

2

1 This is my classroom. Look! A window, a door, chairs and desks. The cupboard is grey and the door is white.

2 This is the playground.

3 Look! Four students.

4 This is my teacher.

Writing

3 Count the words. Then write the numbers.

1 This is my classroom. [4]
(1 2 3 4)

2 A window, a door, chairs and desks. [ ]

3 Look! Four students. [ ]

4 This is my teacher, Mrs Brown. [ ]

4 Write your ideas.

My classroom

Classroom object	Colour
door	______
desk	______
chair	______
window	______

5 Read. Then write for you and draw.

This is my classroom.
This is the door. It's blue.
This is the desk. It's brown.
This is the chair. It's red.
This is the window. It's white.

This is ______

1 Review

1 Write. clock teacher ~~board~~ chair playground desk

1
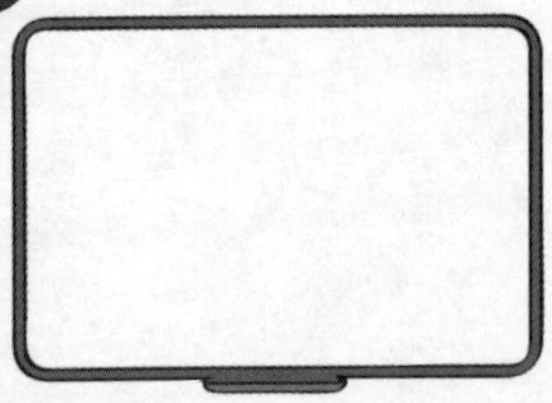

2

3

1		b	o	a	r	d				
2				t						
				m						
3				y						
4				s						
				c						
5				h						
				o						
				o						
6				l						

4
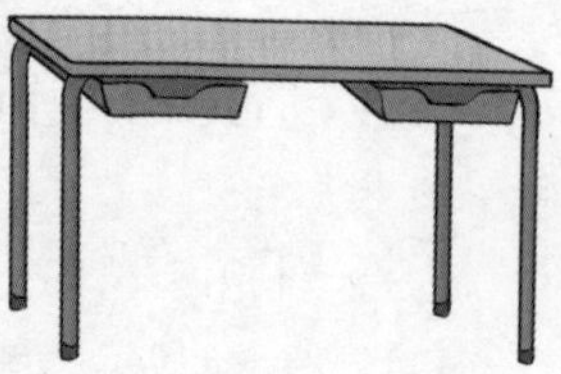

5

6

2 Circle the odd one out. Then write.

1 pink blue (teacher) red teacher

2 student clock bin desk ______

3 green chair white black ______

4 seven three four classroom ______

5 purple two ten eight ______

6 window door board nine ______

3 Write.

1 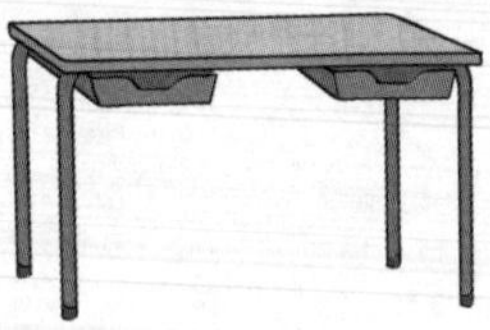
2 
3 
4 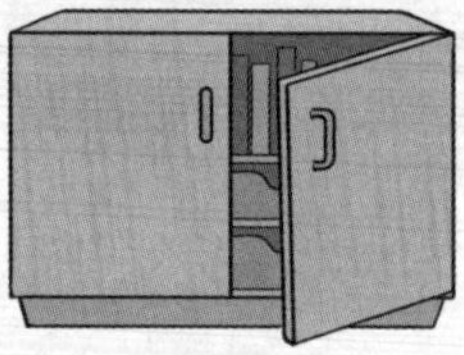

1 What is it? It's a cupboard.

2 __________ is it? It's __________.

3 __________? __________

4 __________? __________

4 Read and circle. Then colour.

1 It's a door. It's orange.

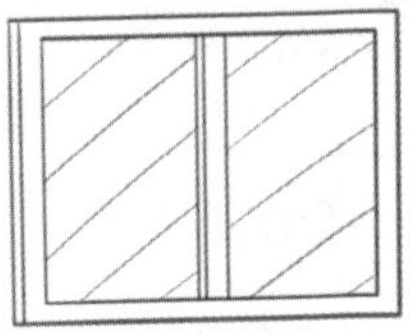
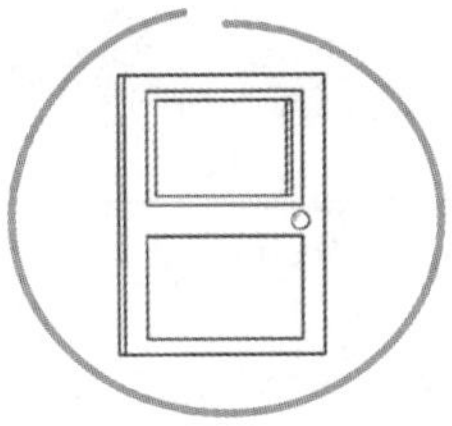

2 It's a cupboard. It's brown.

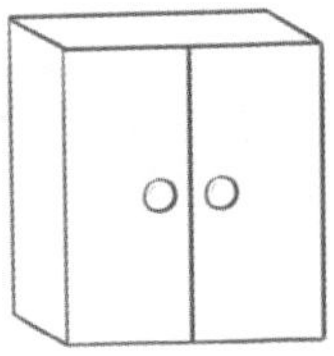
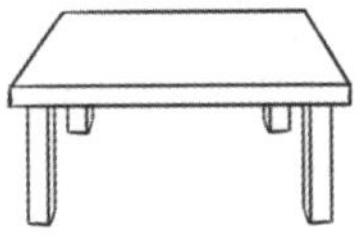

3 It's a clock. It's yellow.

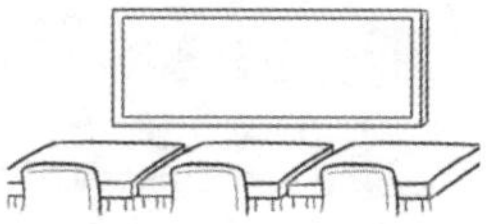

4 It's a bin. It's grey.

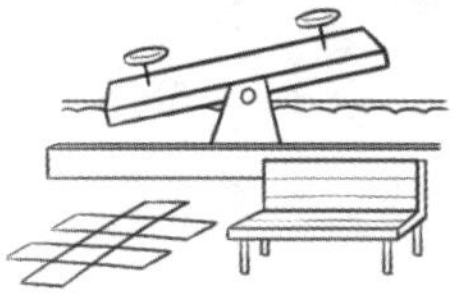

Unit 1 My progress ✓

I can talk about classroom objects.	✔	✔	✔
I can ask and answer *What is it?*	✔	✔	✔
I can talk about the colour of things.	✔	✔	✔
I can read a story.	✔	✔	✔
I can write about my school.	✔	✔	✔
I can make and play a board game.	✔	✔	✔

My effort

Excellent!

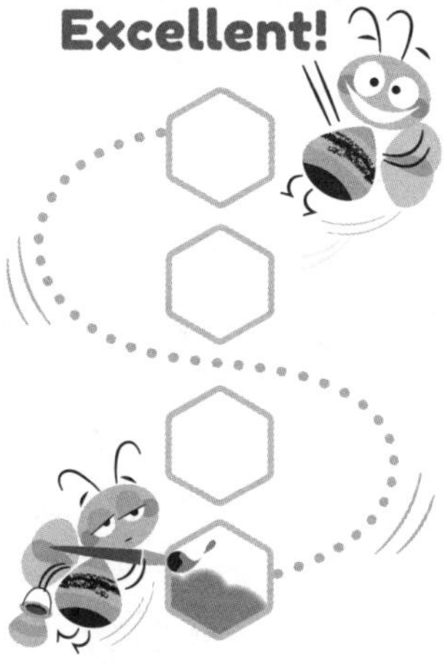

2 My things
Lesson 1 Words

1 Read and number.

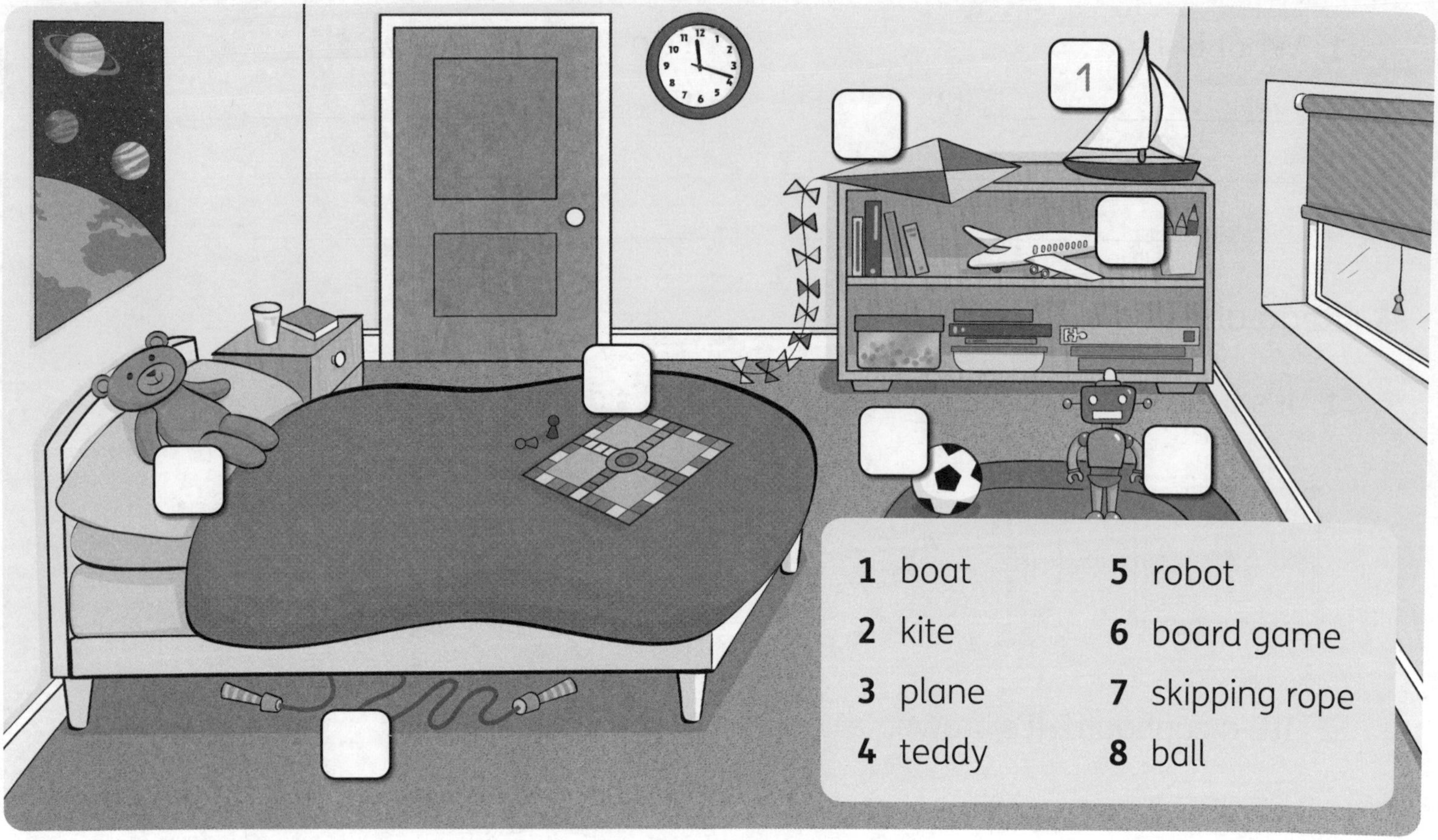

2 Write.

1  skipping rope

2  ______________________

3  ______________________

4  ______________________

5 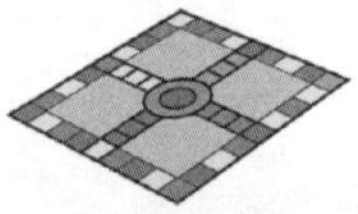 ______________________

6  ______________________

7  ______________________

8  ______________________

3 What is it? Write.

1 

It's a boat.

2 

3 

4 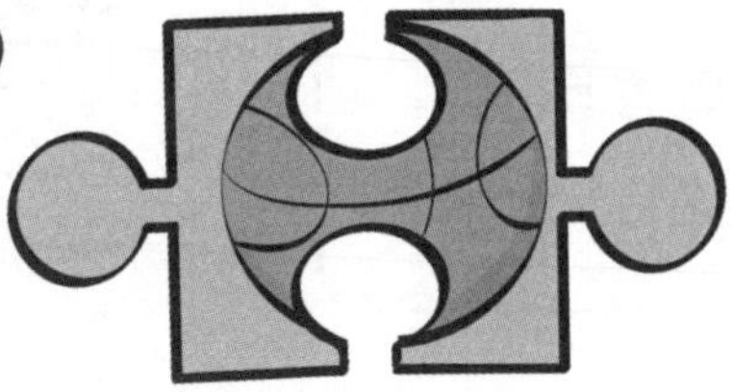

5 

6 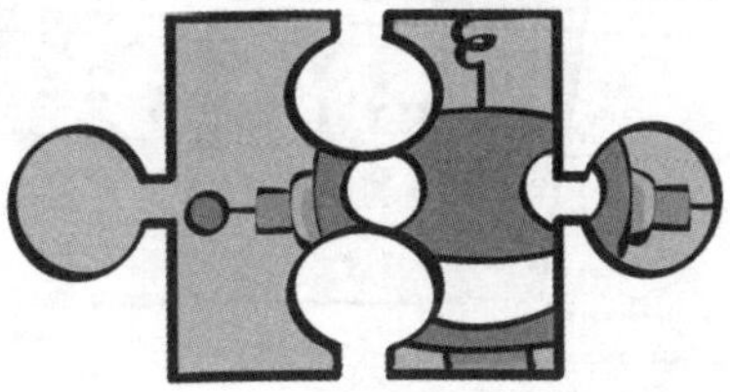

4 Write.

1 What's your favourite toy?

It's a board game.

2 What's your favourite toy?

3 What's your favourite toy?

4 What's your favourite toy?

5 What's your favourite toy?

6 What's your favourite toy?

1 Read and circle.

1 I've got / I haven't got a boat.
2 I've got / I haven't got a kite.
3 I've got / I haven't got a plane.
4 I've got / I haven't got a teddy.
5 I've got / I haven't got a ball.
6 I've got / I haven't got a robot.

2 Read and write *A* (Anna) or *P* (Peter).

1 I haven't got a kite. A
2 I've got a teddy. ____
3 I've got a robot. ____
4 I haven't got a board game. ____
5 I've got a ball. ____
6 I've got a skipping rope. ____

3 Write. **'ve got** **haven't got**

1

I ________________ a boat.

2

I ________________ a plane.

3

I ________________ ball.

4 Read and write the names.

Lea: I haven't got a ball. I've got a robot. I've got a kite.

Dina: I've got a plane. I haven't got a boat. I've got a ball.

Emma: I've got a board game. I've got a teddy. I haven't got a kite.

Aisha: I've got a board game. I've got a skipping rope. I haven't got a plane.

1 

______

2 

Lea

3 

______

4 

______

5 Write.

1 

I've got a ball.
I haven't got
a ______.

2 

______

3 

______

➔ Go to Grammar check page 125

1 Find and circle.

1

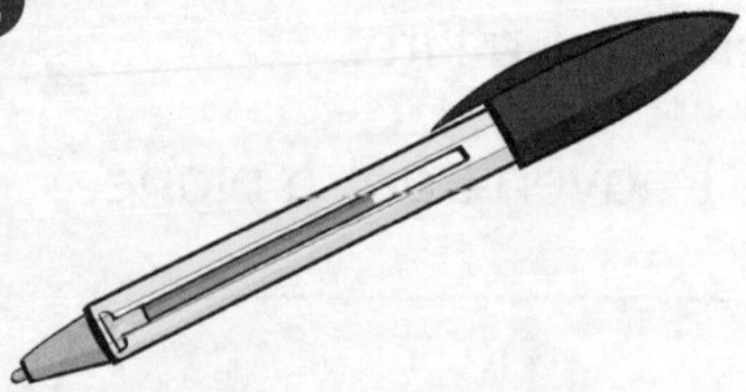

rupenker

2

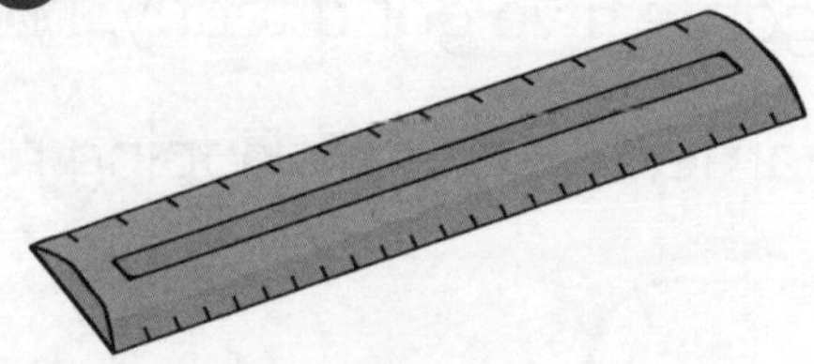

barulerod

3

adbooker

4

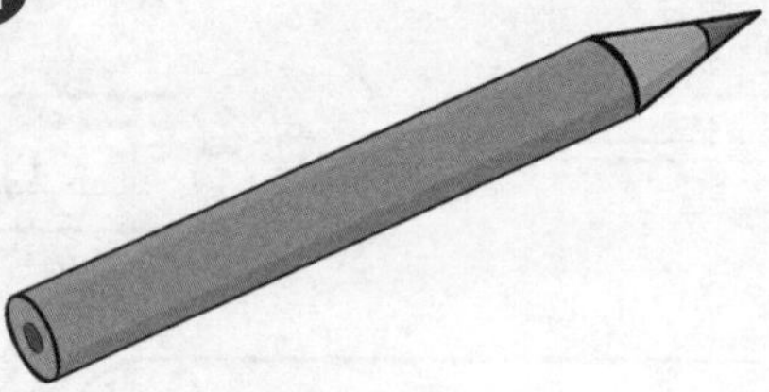

opencilus

5

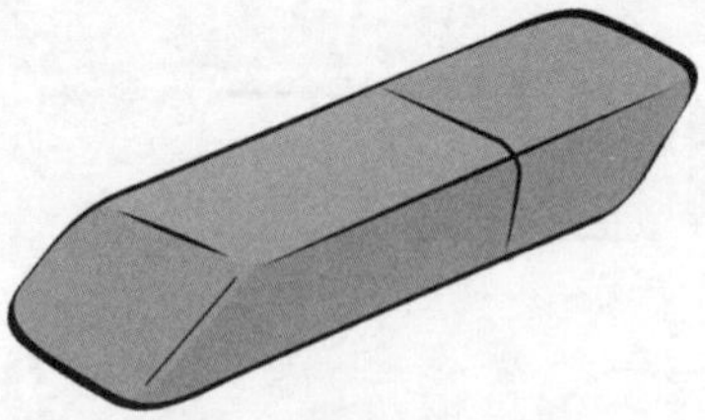

etrubberes

6

ruybagit

2 Write.

I've got **I haven't got**

bag **book** ~~**pen**~~ **pencil** **rubber** **ruler**

1 I haven't got a pen.
2 ______
3 ______
4 ______
5 ______
6 ______

3 Read and write the letter.

1 This is your book. f

2 This is your bag. ___

3 This is my ruler. ___

4 This is your ruler. ___

5 This is my book. ___

6 This is my bag. ___

a

b

c

d

e

f

4 Write Maria's sentences.

This is my   **This is your**

1 This is your  pen.

2 ___  ___

3 ___  ___

4 ___  ___

5 ___  ___

6 ___  ___

➜ Go to Grammar check page 125

1 Look at the pictures. What school things can you see?

2 Read the story.

Serena and Yuma's school things

3 Read again and number.

1 I haven't got my bag!

2 Here. I've got my book.

3 This is your pencil.

4 This is my teddy.

5 Here, Yuma. I've got a robot.

a 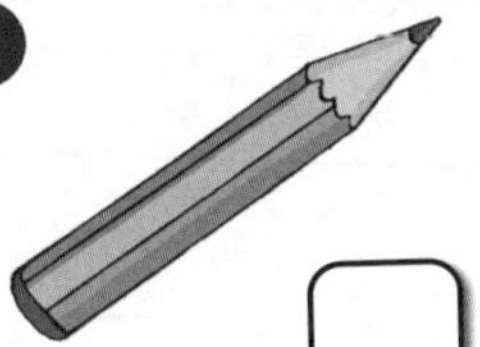 ☐

b  ☐

c 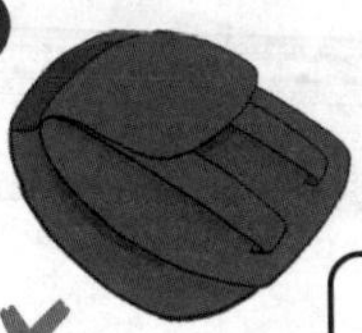 ✗ 1

d  ☐

e 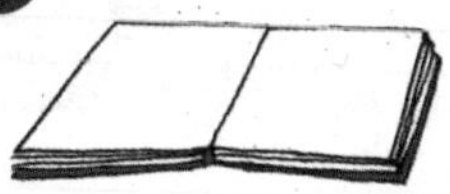 ☐

4 Order the words.

1 

my | haven't | I | book! | got

I haven't ______________________________

2 

toy. | got | I | haven't | a

____

3 

favourite | toy. | It's | my

____

5 Circle, tick ✔ and colour.

1 **Circle.**
My favourite part of the story is

1 2 3
4 5 6

2 **Tick ✔.**
My favourite character is

 ☐  ☐

3 **Colour.**
How many stars for the story?

Reading

1 Write. **skateboard** **bat** ~~**baseball**~~ **scooter**

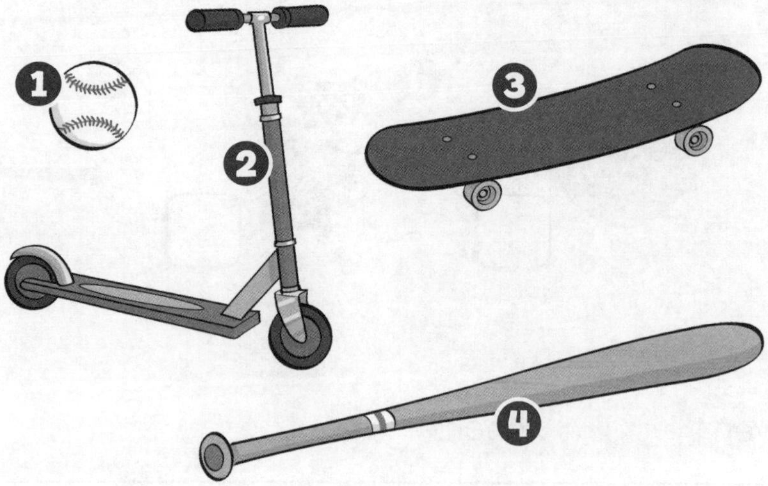

1 baseball

2 ______________

3 ______________

4 ______________

2 Read and tick ✔ picture 1, 2 or 3.

Dear Harper,
This is my toy box.
In my toy box I've got a bat. I've got a baseball.
I've got a skipping rope, too.
I haven't got a scooter. I haven't got a skateboard.
This is my favourite toy. It's my robot.
What's your favourite toy?
From,
Ethan

1

2

3

Writing

3 Circle the words.

1 I ' v e g o t a b a t .

2 I ' v e g o t a s k i p p i n g r o p e , t o o .

3 I h a v e n ' t g o t a s c o o t e r .

4 T h i s i s m y f a v o u r i t e t o y .

4 Tick ✔ or cross ✘ your things. **I've got = ✔ I haven't got = ✘**

plane	☐	robot	☐	kite	☐	skipping rope	☐
boat	☐	baseball	☐	ball	☐	skateboard	☐
scooter	☐	bat	☐	teddy	☐	board game	☐

5 Read. Then write for you and draw.

I've got a skateboard.
I've got a scooter, too.
I haven't got a plane.
I haven't got a robot.
My favourite toy is my kite.

I've got ______________________

____

____

____

____

____

2 Review

1 Find, circle and write.

1

boat

2

3

g	p	l	a	n	e	b
b	t	f	m	u	q	j
o	r	o	b	o	t	k
a	v	r	w	y	s	i
t	e	d	d	y	b	t
b	l	k	c	f	j	e
p	e	n	c	i	l	r

4

5

6

2 Read. Then circle the odd one out.

1 pen pencil robot rubber
2 robot ruler teddy ball
3 scooter bat baseball bag
4 pen scooter rubber ruler
5 kite pencil board game boat
6 teddy pen ruler rubber

3 Read and number.

1 I've got a book. I haven't got a kite.
2 I've got a skateboard. I haven't got a skipping rope.
3 I haven't got a book. I've got a kite.
4 I haven't got a skateboard. I've got a skipping rope.

a

b

c

d

1

4 Write. ✔ = **I've got** ✘ = **I haven't got**

1 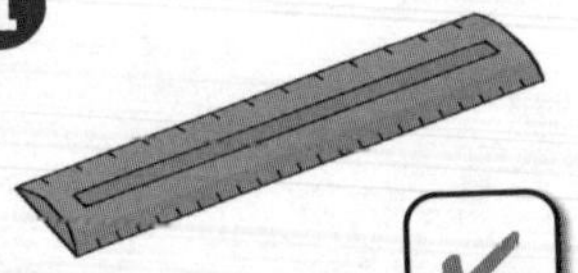 ✔ I've got a ruler.

2 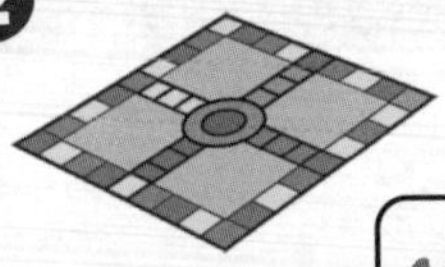 ✔ ______________________

3 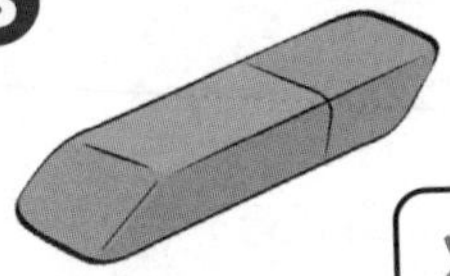 ✘ ______________________

4  ✘ ______________________

5  ✘ ______________________

6  ✔ ______________________

5 Write. **my** **your**

1 

This is ________ skipping rope.

2 

This is ________ teddy.

3 

This is ________ bat.

Unit 2 My progress ✔

I can talk about toys.	✔	✔	✔
I can use *I've got* and *I haven't got*.	✔	✔	✔
I can talk about my and your school things.	✔	✔	✔
I can read a story.	✔	✔	✔
I can write about my toys and games.	✔	✔	✔
I can make a block chart of my favourite toys.	✔	✔	✔

My effort

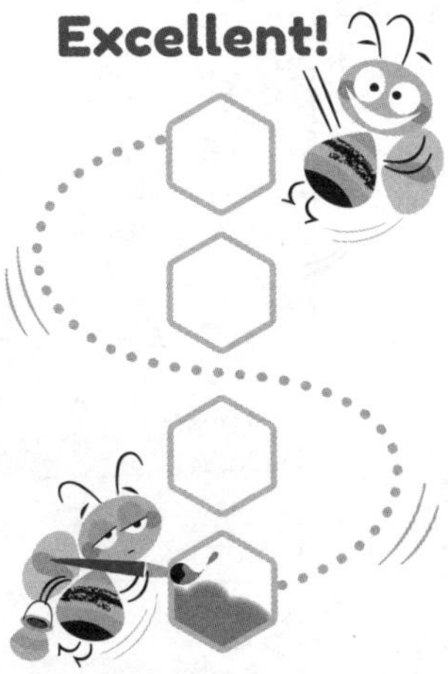

3 Fun with friends

Lesson 1 Words

1 Read and match.

1 read
2 play tennis
3 draw
4 climb

5 sing
6 dance
7 play basketball
8 play football

2 Write.

play tennis

3 Which letters are missing? Write. **a e i o u**

1 

pl_a_y f_o__o_tb_a_ll

2 

pl___y b___sk___tb___ll

3 

pl___y t___nn___s

4 

r______d

5 

dr___w

6 

d___nc___

4 Write.

1 

2 

3 

4 

3 Lesson 2 Grammar

1 Read and circle.

I **can** / **can't** play football.

I **can** / **can't** play tennis.

I **can** / **can't** play basketball.

I **can** / **can't** sing.

I **can** / **can't** climb.

I **can** / **can't** dance.

2 Write. **can** **can't**

1 I ___can't___ draw.

2 I ______________ dance.

3 I ______________ read.

4 I ______________ climb.

5 I ______________ sing.

3 Read and match.

1 I can play football.
I can't play basketball.

2 I can play basketball.
I can't play tennis.

3 I can play tennis.
I can't dance.

4 I can dance.
I can't play football.

a

b
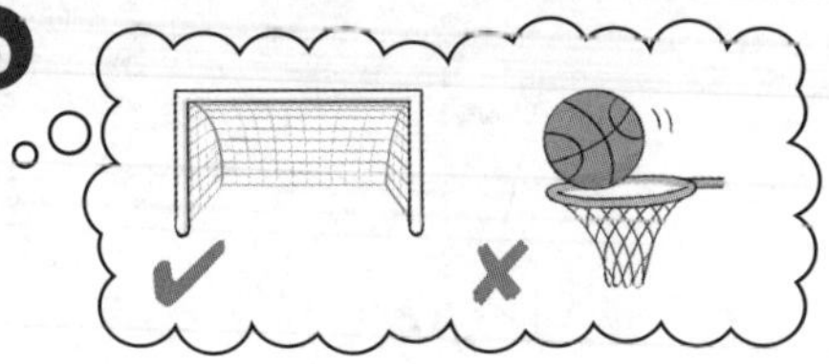

c
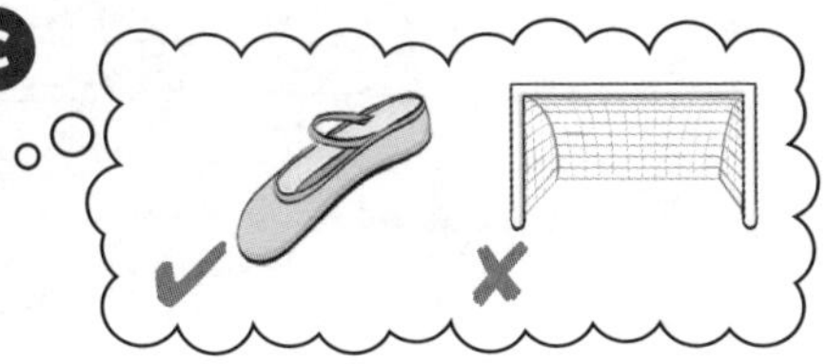

d

4 Tick ✔ what you can do and cross ✘ what you can't do. Write.

1

[✔]
I can play football.

2
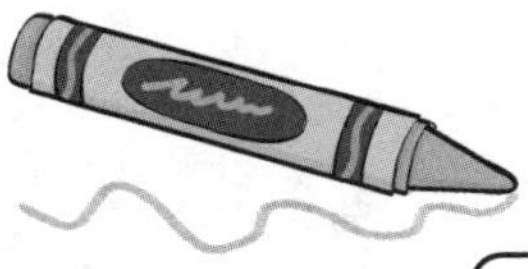
[ ]
____

3

[ ]
____

4

[ ]
____

5

[ ]
____

6

[ ]
____

7

[ ]
____

8

[ ]
____

➔ Go to Grammar check page 126

3 Lesson 3 Words and Grammar

1 Look, read and number.

catch	
fly	1
jump	
run	
swim	
talk	

2 What can you do? Draw ☺ or ☹. Then write.

can can't

1

I can run.

2

3
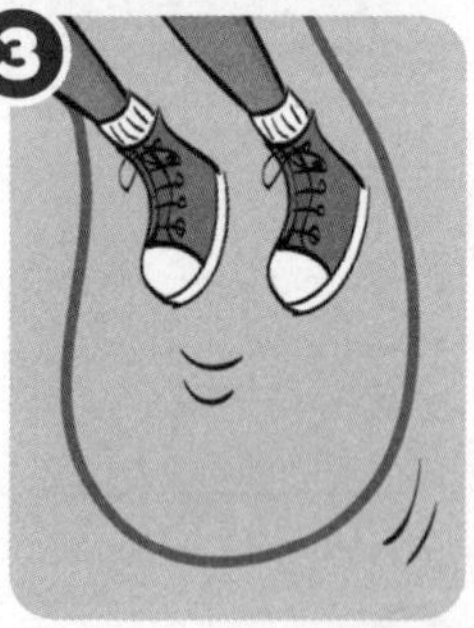

4
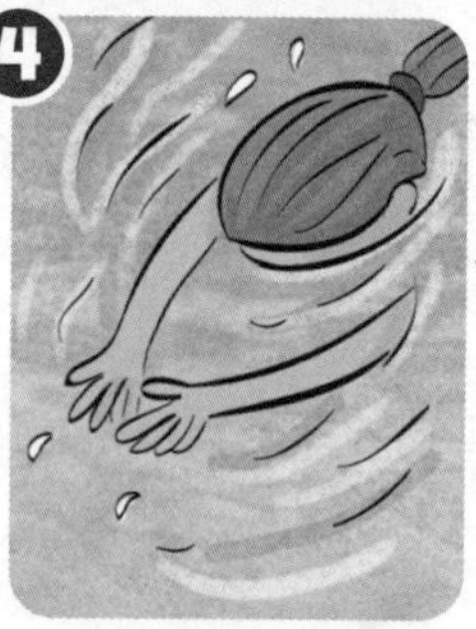

5

6

3 Read and circle.

1

Can you run?

a Yes, I can.
b No, I can't.

2

Can you catch?

a Yes, I can.
b No, I can't.

3

Can you swim?

a Yes, I can.
b No, I can't.

4

Can you jump?

a Yes, I can.
b No, I can't.

5

Can you talk?

a Yes, I can.
b No, I can't.

6

Can you fly?

a Yes, I can.
b No, I can't.

4 Order the words.

1 catch? you Can

Can you catch?

Yes, can. I

______

2 you fly? Can

______

can. I Yes,

______

3 you Can swim?

______

I No, can't.

______

4 Can run? you

______

can't. No, I

______

➜ Go to Grammar check page 126

1 Look at the pictures. What actions can you see?

2 Read the story.

Pip the penguin

3 Read again. Write *T* (true) or *F* (false).

1 
I can catch. T

2 
I can dance. ____

3 
I can fly. ____

4 
I can jump. ____

4 Read again and write.

jump No ~~can~~ can't

1 
I __can__ run.

2 
________, I can't.

3 
Penguins ________ fly.

4 
I can ________!

5 Circle, tick ✔ and colour.

1 **Circle.**
My favourite part of the story is

1 2 3

4 5 6

2 **Tick ✔.**
My favourite character is

☐ ☐

3 **Colour.**
How many stars for the story?

3 Lesson 5 Skills and Culture

Reading

1 Find and circle. Then write.

i c e s k a t e m a k e a s n o w m a n s k i s l e d g e

❶ 

sledge

❷ 

____

❸ 

____

❹ 

____

____

2 Read and number.

❶
FROM Jessie.xyz@oup.com
SUBJECT Free time

Hi Zach,
Can you dance?
I can dance. It's my favourite free time activity. I can jump, but I can't climb. I can swim, too.
Jessie

❷
FROM Suzy.xyz@oup.com
SUBJECT Free time

Hi Zach,
Can you play football?
It's my favourite free time activity. I can play tennis, but I can't play basketball. I can climb.
Suzy

❸
FROM Holly.xyz@oup.com
SUBJECT Free time

Hi Zach,
I can make a snowman. I can sledge, but I can't ski. I can't ice skate.
Can you ice skate?
Holly

ⓐ  ☐

ⓑ  ☐

ⓒ  ☐

Writing

3 Circle each sentence. Then count and write the number.

1 Can you swim? I can swim. It's my favourite activity. 3

2 I can make a snowman, but I can't sledge.

3 Can you jump? I can jump and I can climb.

4 I can ice skate. I can ski, too. Can you ski?

4 Tick ✔ what you can do. Cross ✘ what you can't do.

dance ☐ climb ☐ draw ☐ sing ☐ swim ☐ fly ☐

play basketball ☐ play football ☐ play tennis ☐ jump ☐

catch ☐ run ☐ ski ☐ sledge ☐ make a snowman ☐

5 Read. Then write for you and draw.

I can catch. I can climb.
I can make a snowman.
I can jump, too.
I can't ice skate.
I can't ski.

I can

1 Order the letters.

1 

m l i c b

climb

2 

n i s g

3 

l a t k

4 

t a c h c

5 

p u m j

6 

y l f

7 

d e a r

8 

m s w i

2 Write the words in the boxes.

~~sledge~~ play basketball make a snowman
play tennis ski swim ice skate play football

sledge

3 Write.

1
I can dance.
I can't.

2
I ______.
I ______.

3
I ______.
I ______.

4 Write. **Yes, I can.** **No, I can't.**

1 
Can you run?
No, I can't.

2 
Can you catch?
______

3 
Can you ski?
______

4 
Can you fly?
______

Unit 3 My progress ✓

I can talk about activities.	✓	✓	✓
I can use *I can* and *I can't*.	✓	✓	✓
I can ask and answer about actions.	✓	✓	✓
I can read a story.	✓	✓	✓
I can write about my free time activities.	✓	✓	✓
I can make a trophy for my friend.	✓	✓	✓

My effort

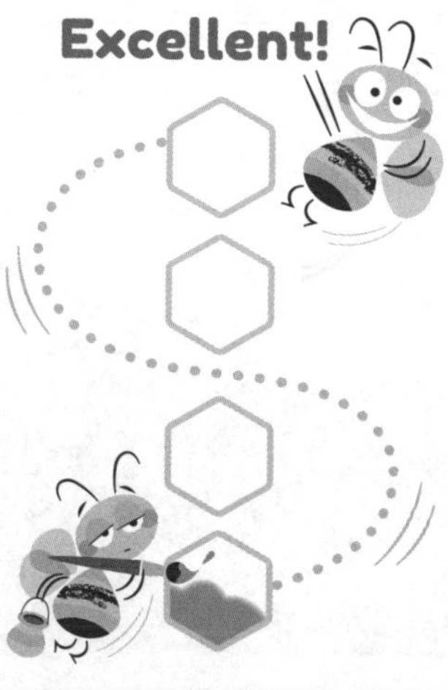

4 Outdoors
Lesson 1 Words

1 What's the animal? Find and colour.

1 

b	e	d	u	c	k	t	e	r

2 

a	e	t	b	e	e	l	h	f

3 

m	l	k	f	i	s	h	v	i

4 

c	i	s	p	i	d	e	r	o	l

5 

c	u	i	f	r	o	g	m	o

6 

o	d	c	a	t	r	f	o	g

7 

l	e	m	d	o	g	p	r	s

8 

g	e	r	s	n	a	k	e	a	l

2 Write.

1 spider
2 ______
3 ______
4 ______
5 ______
6 ______
7 ______
8 ______

3 Write. **can** **can't**

1  swim — A fish can swim.

2  fly — ______________________

3  run — ______________________

4  talk — ______________________

5  dance — ______________________

6  climb — ______________________

4 Write. **Yes, it can.** **No, it can't.**

1 

Can a cat read?
No, it can't.

2 
Can a spider climb?
____

3 
Can a dog catch?
____

4 
Can a snake talk?
____

5 
Can a frog fly?
____

6 
Can a duck swim?
____

1 Read and circle.

1 Is it a bee?
(Yes, it is.)
No, it isn't.

2 Is it a duck?
Yes, it is.
No, it isn't.

3 Is it a snake?
Yes, it is.
No, it isn't.

4 Is it a cat?
Yes, it is.
No, it isn't.

5 Is it a spider?
Yes, it is.
No, it isn't.

6 Is it a frog?
Yes, it is.
No, it isn't.

2 What's next? Write. **Yes, it is.** **No, it isn't.**

1 Is it a spider?
Yes, it is.

2 Is it a duck?
______

3 Is it a cat?
______

4 Is it a fish?
______

3 Guess and write questions. Then join the dots and tick ✔ or cross ✘.

1
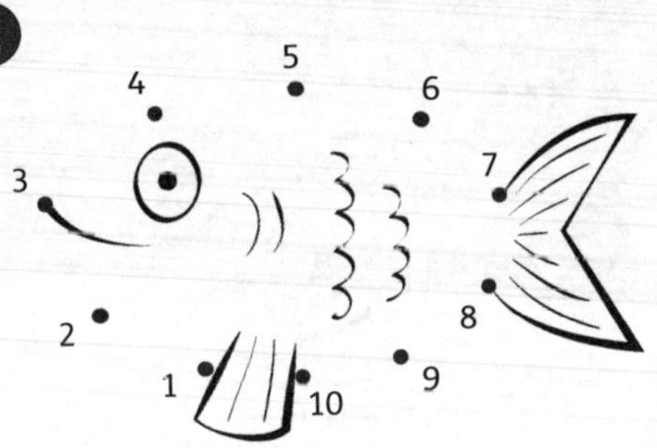

2

3

Is it a fish? ✔

________ ☐

________ ☐

4
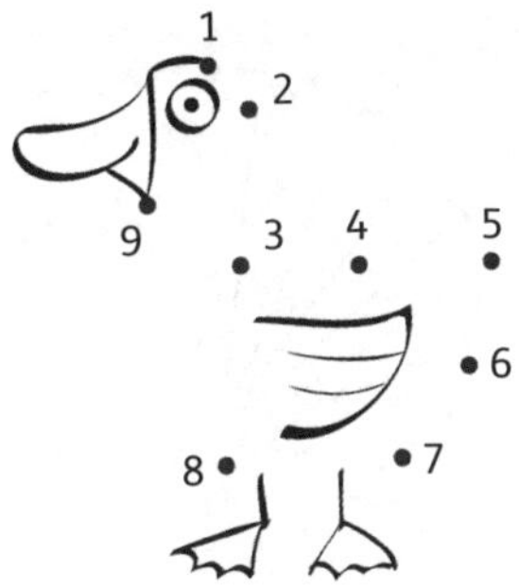

5
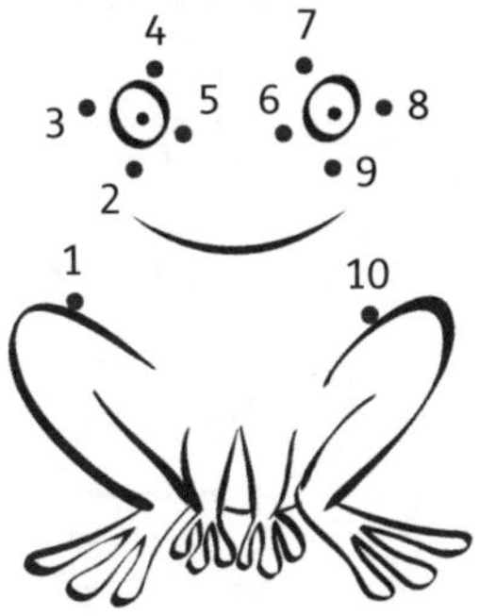

6
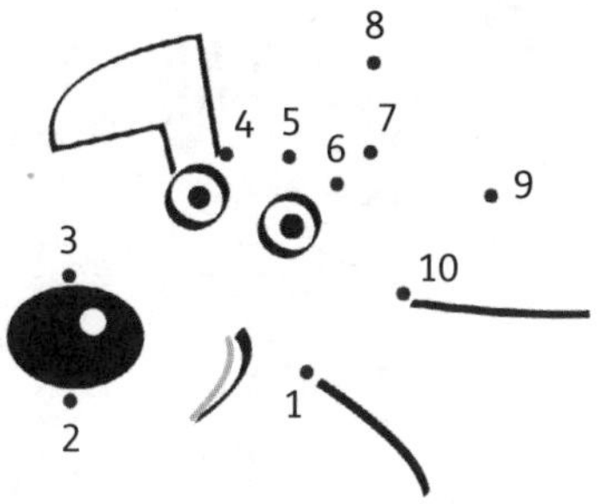

________ ☐

________ ☐

________ ☐

4 Write the questions. Then answer.

Yes, it is. **No, it isn't.**

1

2

3

➜ Go to Grammar check page 127

1 Trace and write.

beach ~~**flower**~~ **lake** **plant** **shell** **tree**

1 

flower

2 

3 

4 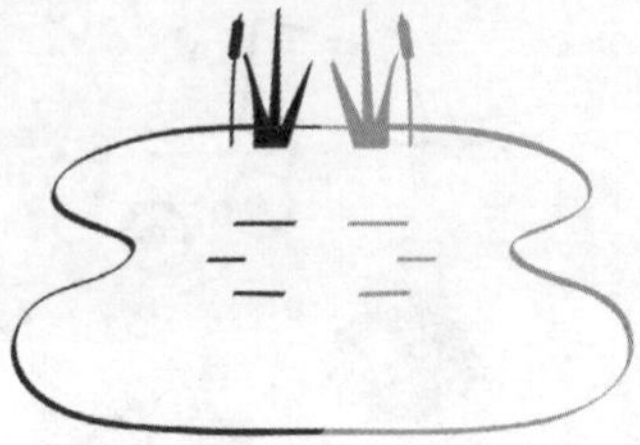

5 

6 

2 Write.

Yes, it is. **No, it isn't.**

1 

Is it a plant? No, it isn't.

2 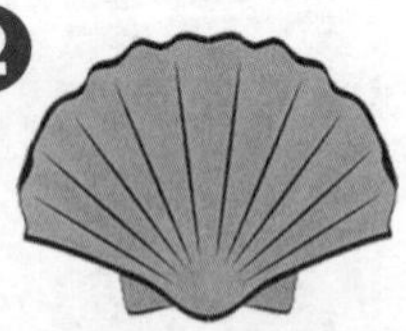

Is it a shell? ____________

3 

Is it a lake? ____________

4 

Is it a flower? ____________

3 Read and circle.

1

There's / There are
some shells.

2

There's / There are
a flower.

3

There's / There are
some plants.

4

There's / There are
a lake.

5

There's / There are
some trees.

6

There's / There are
a beach.

4 Write. **There's a** **There are some**

1 There's a beach.
2 ______ shells.
3 ______ tree.
4 ______ lake.
5 ______ plants.
6 ______ flowers.

→ Go to Grammar check page 127

1 Look at the pictures. What animals can you see?

2 Read the story.

A great team

3 Read again. Who says it? Match.

1 It's a cat.

2 Can it jump?

3 We're a great team.

4 There's a lake. There's a house.

4 Read and write.

isn't **No** **you** ~~**Is**~~ **Can** **can't**

1

Is it a dog?

No, it ______.

2

______ it jump?

No, it ______.

3

Can ______ swim?

______, I can't.

5 Circle, tick ✔ and colour.

1 **Circle.**
My favourite part of the story is

1 2 3
4 5 6

2 **Tick ✔.**
My favourite character is

☐  ☐ 

☐  ☐ 

3 **Colour.**
How many stars for the story?

4 Lesson 5 Skills and Culture

Reading

1 Write. **sandcastle** **sun** **sea** ~~**sand**~~

❶ 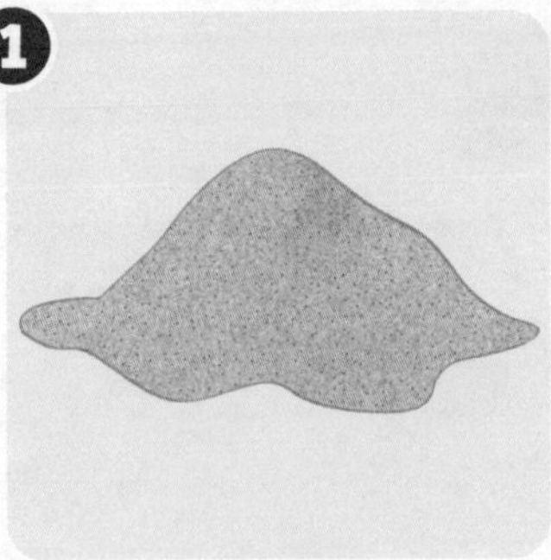

sand

❷ 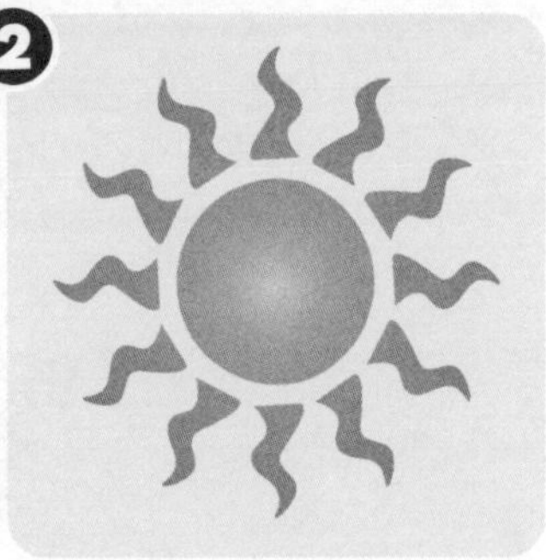

___

❸ 

___

❹ 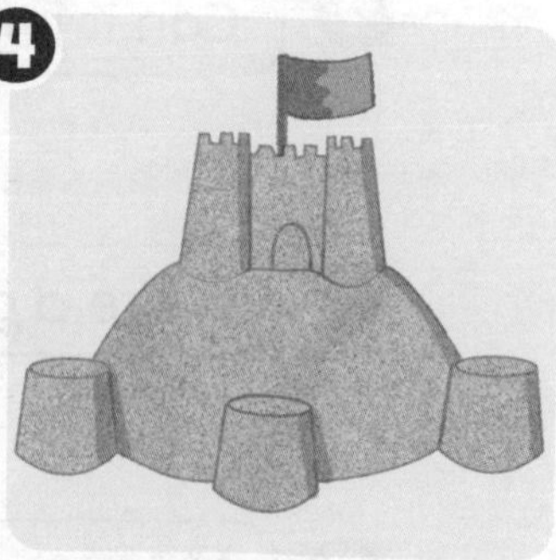

___

2 Read. Then write and match.

Dear Tilly,

I'm at the beach. Can you see the sea? It's blue. Can you see the sun? It's yellow. There's a fish in the sea. It's red. There's a sandcastle. There are some shells on the beach, too. This is my favourite shell. It's white. I can swim in the sea. I can run on the sand.

From,
Charlie

1 What colour is the e a s ___sea___?
2 What colour is the s n u ______?
3 What colour is the s f i h ______?
4 What colour is the h e l l s ______?

a It's red.
b It's white.
c It's blue.
d It's yellow.

Writing

3 Circle the capital letters and full stops.

1 I'm at the beach.
2 This is my favourite shell.
3 It's white.
4 I can run on the sand.

4 Choose and tick ✔ the sea or a lake. Circle what you can see.

sea ☐

lake ☐

sand tree flower shell beach
sandcastle sand plant sun
duck frog fish spider bee

5 Read. Then write for you and draw.

I'm at the lake.
There's a duck. It's green.
There are some trees.
I can run.
I can swim, too.

I'm ______

4 Review

1 Circle the odd one out. Then write.

1 cat dog duck lake — lake
2 bee spider plant frog — ______
3 sand dog sea sandcastle — ______
4 duck sun bee fish — ______
5 shell beach spider tree — ______

2 Write.

Yes, it is. **No, it isn't.**

1  Is it a spider? Yes, it is.

2  Is it a snake? ______

3  Is it a frog? ______

4  Is it a flower? ______

5  Is it a shell? ______

3 Write the questions. Then answer.

1 

2 

4 Look, read and match.

a

d

b

e

c

f

1 There's a flower.
2 There are some plants.
3 There's a shell.
4 There are some shells.
5 There's a plant.
6 There are some flowers.

5 Order the words.

1 lake? a it Is — Is it a lake?
2 bee. It's a — ______
3 some are spiders. There — ______
4 a tree. There's — ______

Unit 4 My progress ✓

I can talk about animals.	✓	✓	✓
I can ask and answer *Is it a ... ?*	✓	✓	✓
I can talk about nature.	✓	✓	✓
I can read a story.	✓	✓	✓
I can write about nature and animals.	✓	✓	✓
I can make and write a postcard.	✓	✓	✓

My effort

Excellent!

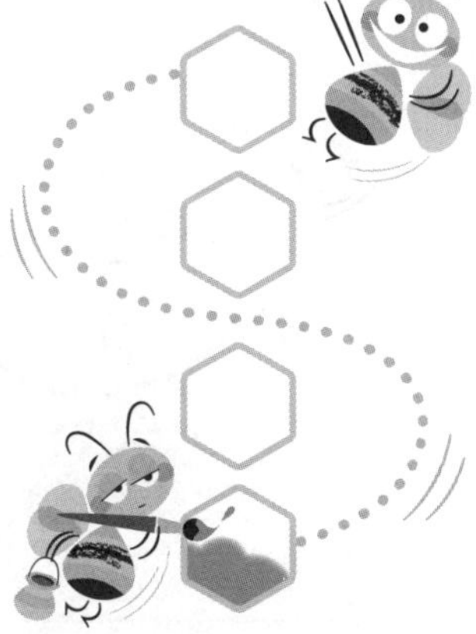

5 My body

Lesson 1 Words

1 Read and number.

face	1
arms	
mouth	
feet	
hands	
eyes	
legs	
body	

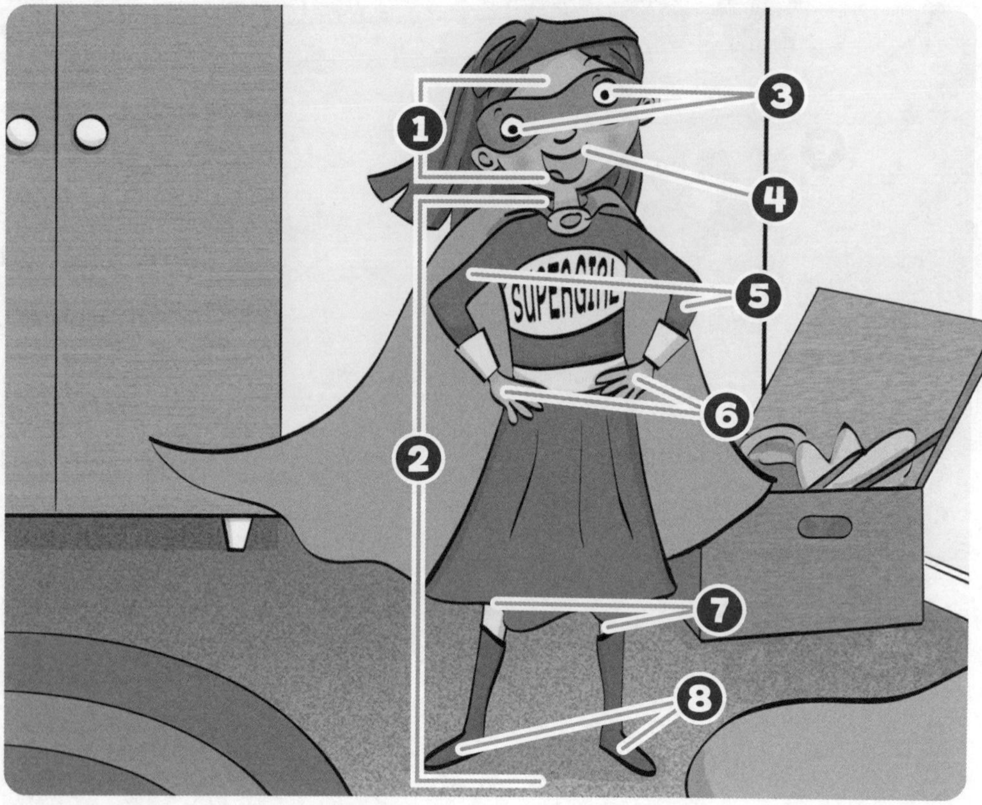

2 Write.

1

eyes

2
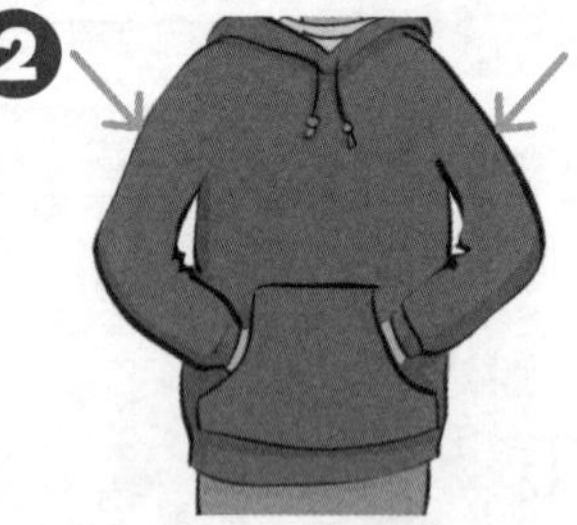

______

3
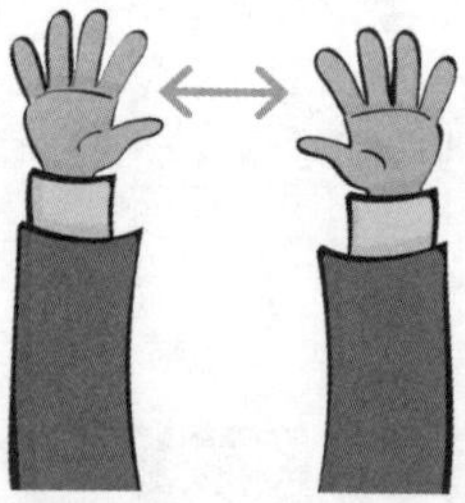

______

4
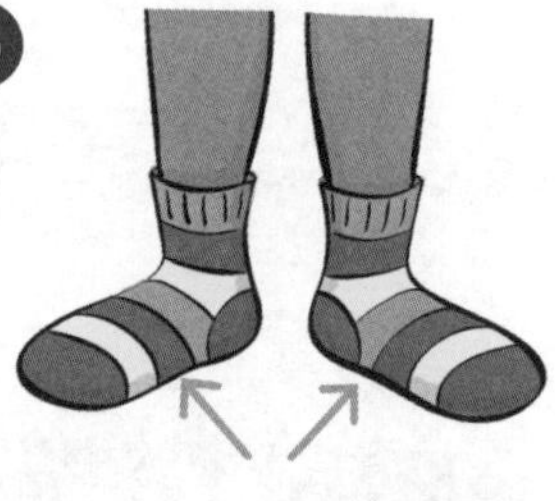

______

5

______

6

______

7

______

8

______

3 Write. **a** **two**

1 I've got a face.

2 I've got two e_______.

3 I've got ______ n_______.

4 I've got ______ a_______.

5 I've got ______ f_______.

6 I've got ______ h_______.

7 I've got ______ m_______.

8 I've got ______ b_______.

4 Read and tick ✔.

1 Touch your eyes!

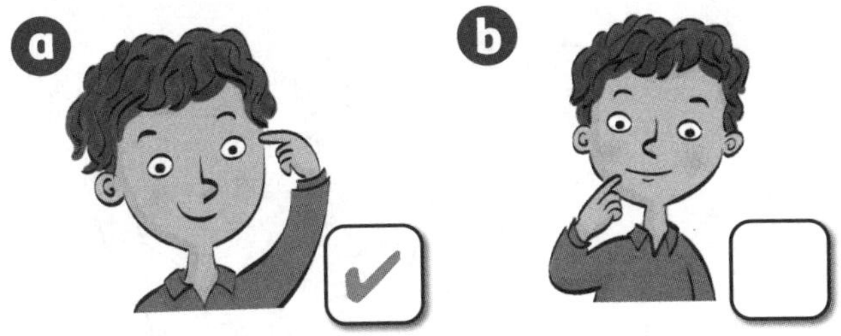

2 Touch your feet!

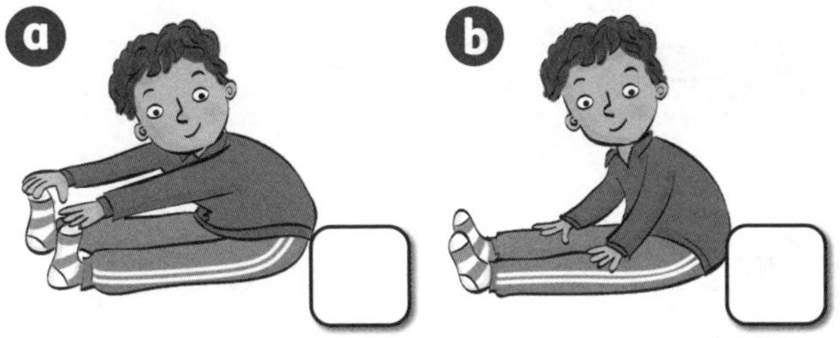

3 Touch your arms!

4 Touch your mouth!

1 Look, read and match. Then circle.

a 

b 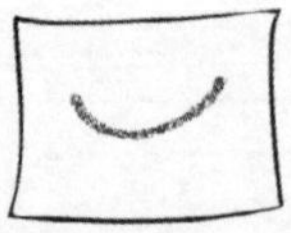

c 

d 

e 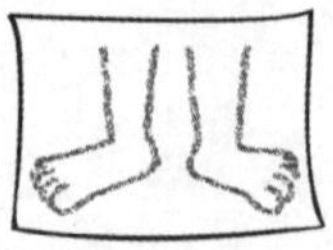

1 This is / **These are** my feet.

2 This is / **These are** my face.

3 This is / **These are** my mouth.

4 This is / **These are** my eyes.

5 This is / **These are** my hands.

2 Write. **This is** **These are**

1 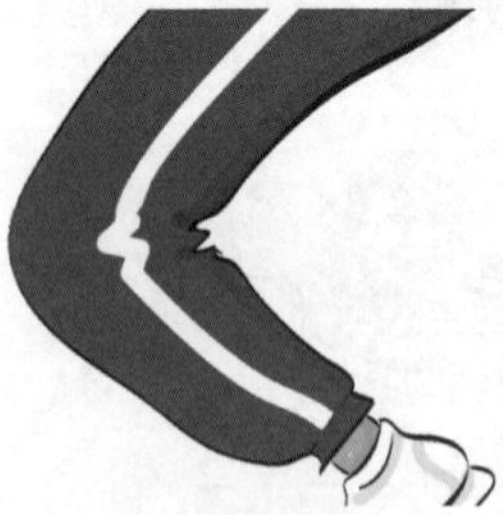

This is my leg.

2 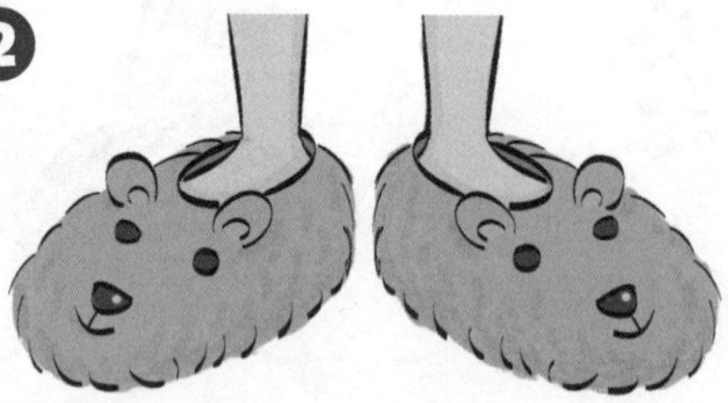

__________ my feet.

3 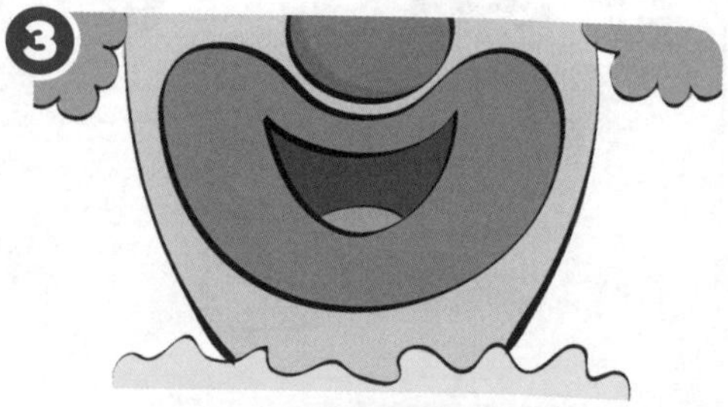

__________ my mouth.

4 

__________ my hands.

5 

__________ my body.

6 

__________ my arms.

3 Read and write *B* (Bongo) or *S* (Scruff).

1 These are my eyes. S
2 This is my eye. ____
3 These are my feet. ____
4 These are my legs. ____
5 This is my mouth. ____
6 These are my hands. ____

4 Write. **These are my** **This is my**

1

These are my eyes.

2
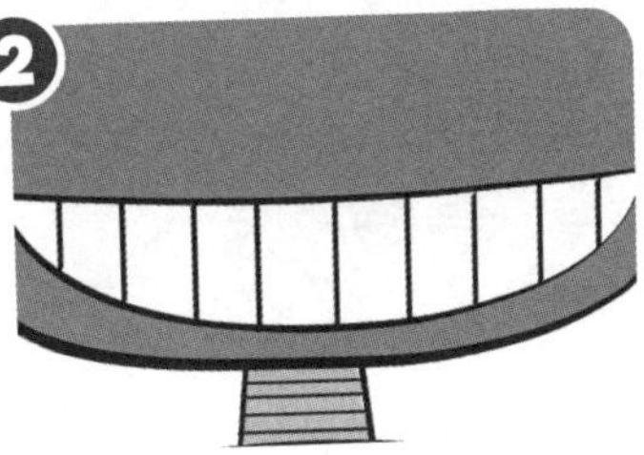
____
____

3
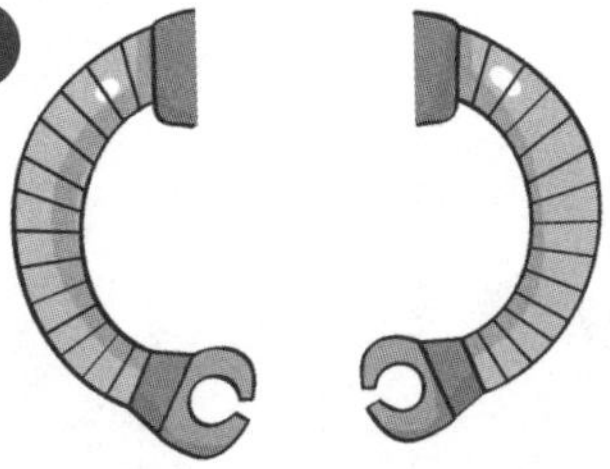
____
____

4

____
____

5
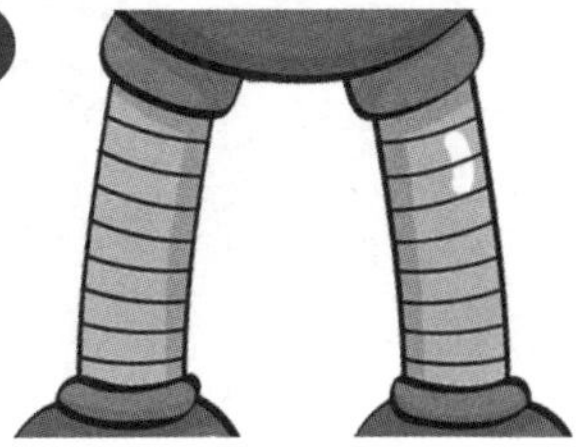
____
____

6

____
____

➔ Go to Grammar check page 128

1 Write. Then find the mystery colour.

head wings tail ~~nose~~ beak ears

1 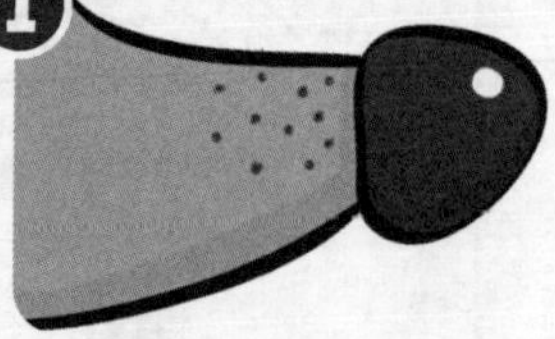

2 

3 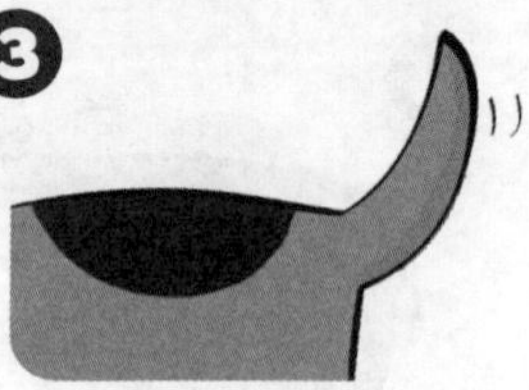

4 

5 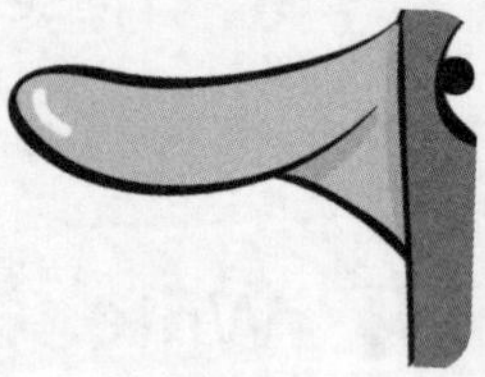

6 

1	n	o	s	e	
2					
3					
4					
5					
6					

The mystery colour is ______________

2 Read and colour.

1 I've got wings. — What colour? — Grey.

2 I've got a beak. — What colour? — Red.

3 I've got ears. — What colour? — Orange.

4 I've got a head. — What colour? — Yellow.

5 I've got a tail. — What colour? — Purple.

3 Look, read and match.

a

b

c

d

e

1 It's got a beak.

2 It's got six legs.

3 It's got a tail.

4 It's got two wings.

5 It's got a nose.

4 Trace and write.

It's got two ears.

It's got four ________.

____

____

____

____

Go to Grammar check page 128

1 Look at the pictures. Which animal body parts can you see?

2 Read the story.

Sam and Sally

3 Read again and match.

1  It's got a nose!

2  Show me your feet.

3  These are my eyes.

a 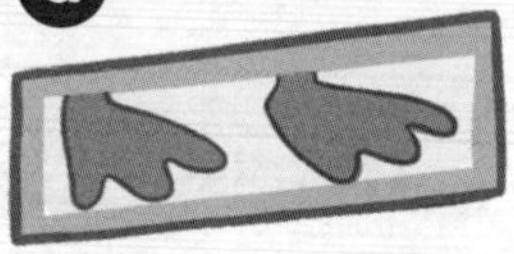

b 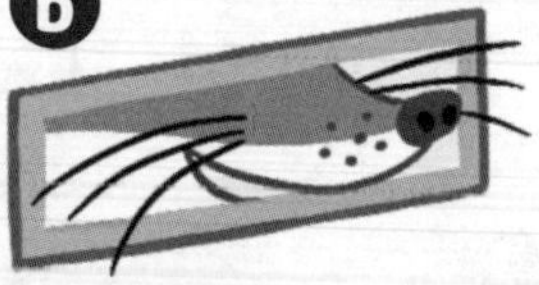

c 

4 Write. **No, you can't come in.** ~~**Open the door!**~~ **Well done.** **Show me your beak.**

1  Open the door!

2  ______________________

3  ______________________

4  ______________________

5 Circle, tick ✔ and colour.

1 **Circle.**
My favourite part of the story is

1 2 3
4 5 6

2 **Tick ✔.**
My favourite character is

☐  ☐ 
☐  ☐ 

3 **Colour.**
How many stars for the story?

5 Lesson 5 Skills and Culture

Reading

1 Write. **lizard** **tortoise** ~~**hamster**~~ **rabbit**

1 

hamster

2 

3 

4 

2 Read and tick ✔ or cross ✘.

1st January

Dear Diary,

I've got a new pet, Dina. It's a rabbit! It's got a white body and black ears. It can jump.

Danny

25th August

Dear Diary,

I want a lizard. My family has got a cat. It's grey. It's got a pink nose. It can play. It's fun, but I want a lizard!

Erin

16th April

Dear Diary,

My family has got a tortoise, Hugo! It's great! It's got four legs and a tail. It's green and brown. They're my favourite colours!

Jay

1 Danny has got a tortoise. ✘

2 Dina is a rabbit. ☐

3 Erin has got a lizard. ☐

4 Hugo has got two legs. ☐

5 The tortoise is green and brown. ☐

6 It's grey. It's a cat. ☐

Writing

3 Circle the capital letters at the start of names.

1 I'm Lucas. I'm from Canada.

2 My mum's name is Marie.

3 This is my hamster, Jasmine.

4 This is my rabbit, Harry.

4 Choose a pet. Circle the body parts.

Favourite pet: ____________________

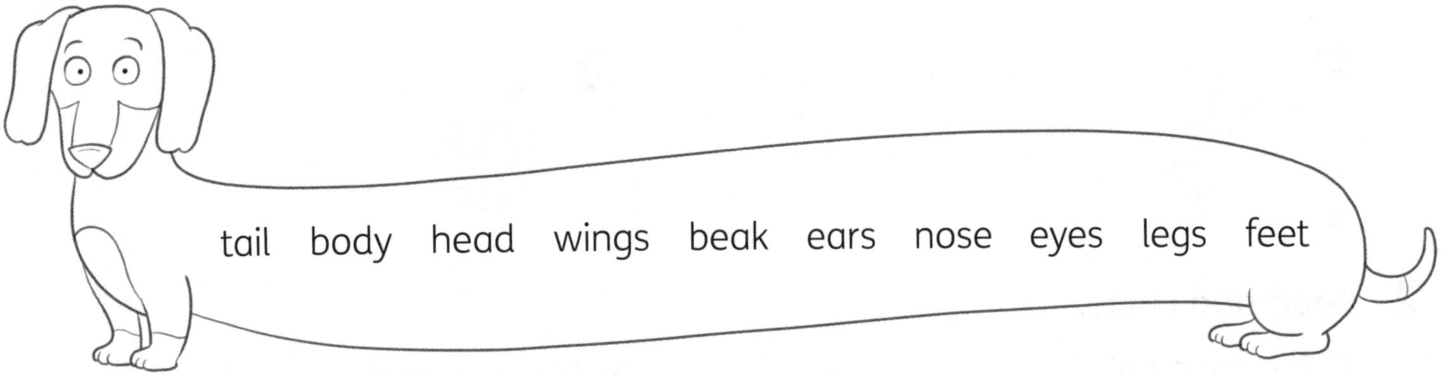

5 Read. Then write about your favourite pet and draw.

This is my dog, Leon.
It's got a brown body.
It's got white feet.
It's got a brown tail.
It can run.

This is ____________________

____

____

____

____

____

1 What's missing? Write.

1  mouth

2  ____________

3  ____________

4  ____________

5  ____________

6  ____________

2 Read and circle.

1 It's got a tail.

2 It's got wings.

3 It's got eight legs.

4 It's got a nose.

3 Write.

1 This is my head.
2 ______________________
3 ______________________
4 ______________________
5 ______________________
6 ______________________

4 Order the words.

1 my | This | face. | is
This is my face.

2 got | It's | eight | eyes.
____

3 are | two | These | hands. | my
____

4 feet. | my | two | are | These
____

5 got | It's | four | legs.
____

Unit 5 My progress ✓

- I can talk about faces and bodies. ✓ ✓ ✓
- I can use *This is my* and *These are my* ✓ ✓ ✓
- I can talk about animals' bodies and faces. ✓ ✓ ✓
- I can read a story. ✓ ✓ ✓
- I can write about pets. ✓ ✓ ✓
- I can design a new animal. ✓ ✓ ✓

My effort

Excellent!

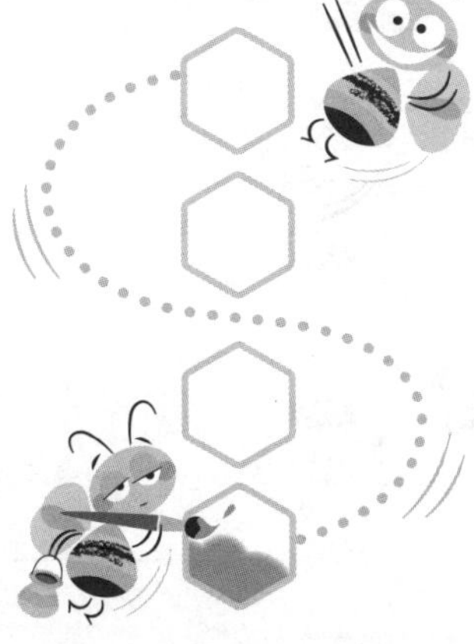

6 My family
Lesson 1 Words

1 Read and number.

Harry's family

1 mum
2 dad
3 sister
4 brother
5 aunt
6 uncle
7 grandma
8 grandpa

2 Find, circle and write.

1  grandma

2  ____________

3  ____________

4  ____________

g	r	a	n	d	m	a
r	b	p	q	b	u	y
a	j	f	h	r	m	u
n	n	w	s	o	z	n
d	a	d	i	t	g	c
p	m	r	s	h	l	l
a	u	n	t	e	t	e
s	d	v	e	r	k	u
b	r	i	r	h	e	r

5  ____________

6  ____________

7  ____________

8  ____________

3 Find and write.

 = brother  = aunt 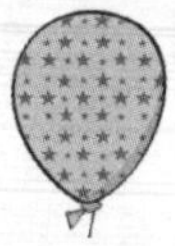 = sister

 = dad  = mum  = uncle

1 This is my uncle.
2 This is my ________.
3 This is my ________.
4 This is my ________.
5 This is my ________.
6 This is my ________.

4 Complete and number.

1 My m_u_m, my d_a_d and my broth_e_r.
2 My gran___ma and my a___nt.
3 My g___ ___ndpa, my mu___ and my da___.
4 My ___um, my ___ad and my un___ ___e.
5 My mu___ and my si___ ___er.

a  [ ]

b  [ ]

c  [1]

d  [ ]

e  [ ]

1 Follow and circle.

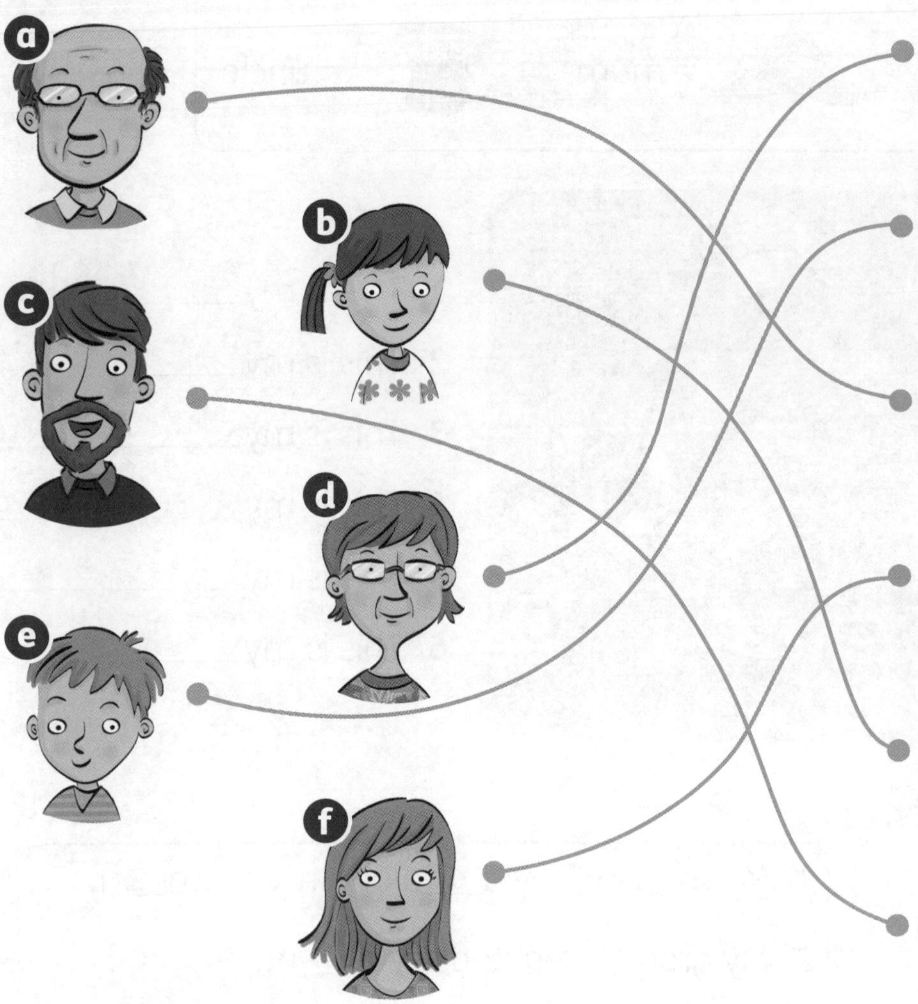

1 She's / He's my grandma.

2 She's / He's my brother.

3 She's / He's my uncle.

4 She's / He's my aunt.

5 She's / He's my sister.

6 She's / He's my dad.

2 Write.

She's He's

1 She's my aunt.

2 ______ my grandpa.

3 ______ my mum.

4 ______ my brother.

5 ______ my uncle.

6 ______ my sister.

3 Look at 2. Who's she? Who's he? Read and match.

1 He's my brother.

2 She's my aunt.

3 She's my mum.

4 He's my grandpa.

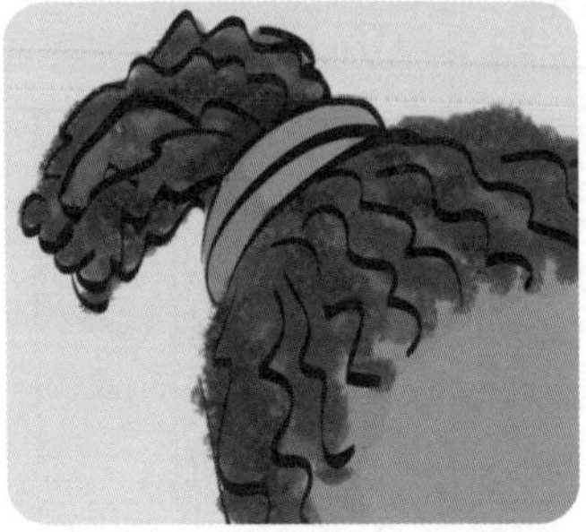

4 Write.

1

Who's she ?

She's my sister.

2

__________ he?

__________ my dad.

3

Who's __________ ?

__________ my grandpa.

4

__________________ ?

______________ grandma.

5

__________________ ?

______________ aunt.

6

__________________ ?

______________ uncle.

➔ Go to Grammar check page 129

1 Write.

1

t h o

1

p a p h y

2

h i r t s y t

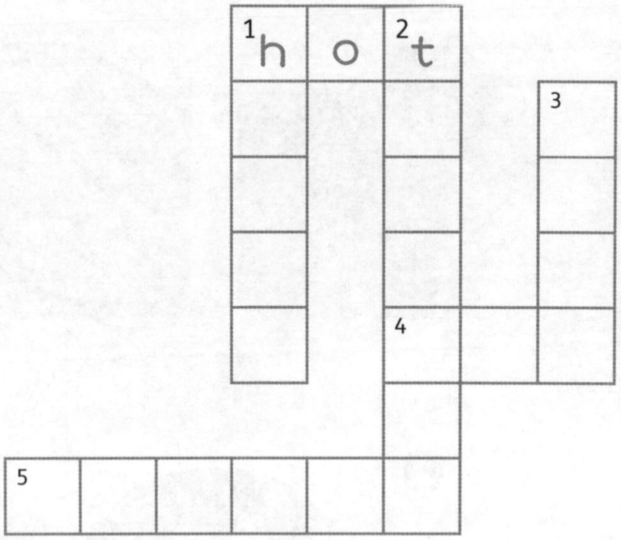

3

d o l c

4

d a s

5

g r u n h y

2 Write.

1 He's thirsty.

2 ______________________

3 ______________________

4 ______________________

5 ______________________

6 ______________________

3 Read and circle.

1

Are you sad?

Yes, I am. / No, I'm not.

2

Are you hungry?

Yes, I am. / No, I'm not.

3

Are you hot?

Yes, I am. / No, I'm not.

4

Are you sad?

Yes, I am. / No, I'm not.

5

Are you thirsty?

Yes, I am. / No, I'm not.

6

Are you cold?

Yes, I am. / No, I'm not.

4 Write.

1

2

3

4

→ Go to Grammar check page 129

6 Lesson 4 Story

1 Look at the pictures. Who's in Mark's family?

2 Read the story.

Moody Mark

3 Read again and write.

1  She's my grandma.

2  He's ______________.

3  ______________

4  ______________

4 Read and number.

1  Let's play a board game.

2  Are you thirsty?

3  Sorry, everyone.

a It's OK. ☐

b No, I'm not. ☐

c No, thanks. ☐

5 Circle, tick ✔ and colour.

1 **Circle.**
My favourite part of the story is

1 2 3
4 5 6

2 **Tick ✔.**
My favourite character is

☐  ☐ 
☐  ☐ 

3 **Colour.**
How many stars for the story?

☆ ☆ ☆ ☆ ☆

Reading

1 Write. **cousins** **boy** ~~**girl**~~ **baby**

1 
girl

2 
____

3 
____

4 
____

2 Read and write the names.

FROM yan.zyx@oup.com TO suyin.zyx@oup.com

Hi Suyin,
I'm Yan. This is my family.
You can see my mum. Her name is Jing.
This is my dad. His name is Chen.
He's my brother. His name is Feng.
He's twelve years old. He's thirsty.
I've got two cousins – one boy and one girl.
The boy is five years old. His name is Jin. He can jump.
The girl is a baby. Her name is Lu.
You can see my grandpa. His name is Yong. He's happy!
Bye! Yan

Yan

____
____

____

____
____

____

Writing

3 Write. **a** **an**

1 I've got ___a___ sister.
2 I've got ________ uncle.
3 I haven't got ________ brother.
4 I haven't got ________ aunt.

4 Circle three people in your family.

mum dad sister brother aunt uncle
cousin baby grandpa grandma

5 Read. Then write for you and draw.

This is my dad.
His name is Carl.
This is my grandma.
Her name is Monica.
This is my sister.
She's ten years old.
Her name is Mia.

This is my ________________

____

____

____

____

____

____

____

6 Review

1 Write the words in the boxes.

~~mum~~ brother girl boy grandma baby
dad uncle aunt sister grandpa cousin

She

mum

He

He or She

2 Read and colour.

thirsty = grey **hot = red** **cold = blue**
hungry = yellow **happy = pink** **sad = purple**

1 

2 

3 

4 

5 

6 

3 Read and match.

1 Are you thirsty?

2 Who's he?

3 Who's she?

a 

b 

c 

4 Read and tick ✔.

1		2		3		4	
It's a girl.	✔	She's cold.	☐	He's happy.	☐	She's my aunt.	☐
It's a boy.	☐	He's cold.	☐	He's sad.	☐	He's my uncle.	☐

5 Write.

I'm not **He's** ~~**Who's**~~ **Are you** **She's** **I am**

1 Who's she?
2 ______________ my cousin.
3 ______________ Uncle Jim!
4 ______________ hungry?
5 No, ______________.
6 Yes, ______________.

Unit 6 My progress ✔

I can talk about family members.	✔	✔	✔
I can ask and answer *Who's he / she?*	✔	✔	✔
I can ask and answer about feelings.	✔	✔	✔
I can read a story.	✔	✔	✔
I can write about my family.	✔	✔	✔
I can make a group book.	✔	✔	✔

My effort

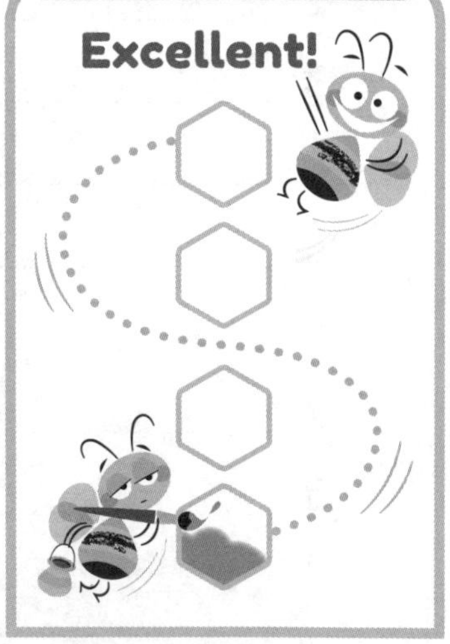

7 My clothes

Lesson 1 Words

1 Read and match.

- jacket
- cap
- trousers
- socks
- hat
- skirt
- shoes
- T-shirt

2 Write.

1 skirt
2 ____________
3 ____________
4 ____________
5 ____________
6 ____________
7 ____________
8 ____________

3 Trace and write.

1
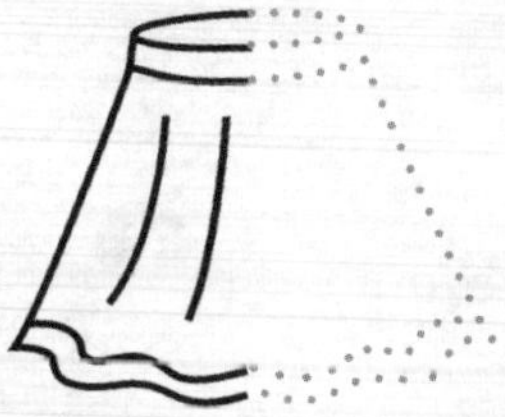

This is my skirt.

2
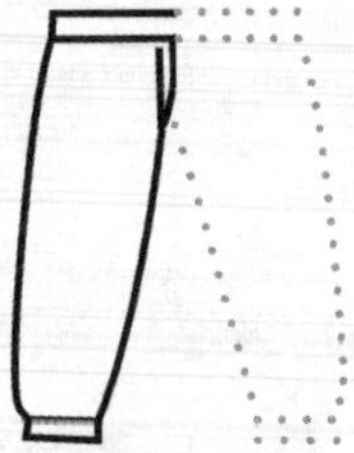

These are my ______.

3
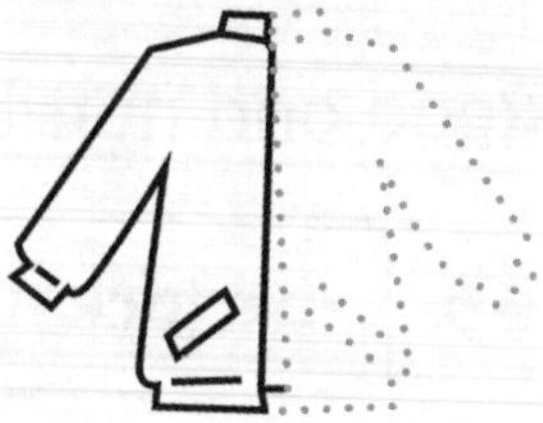

This is my ______.

4
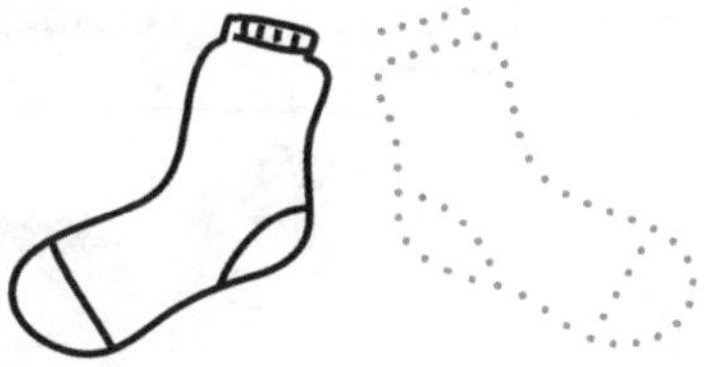

These are my ______.

5
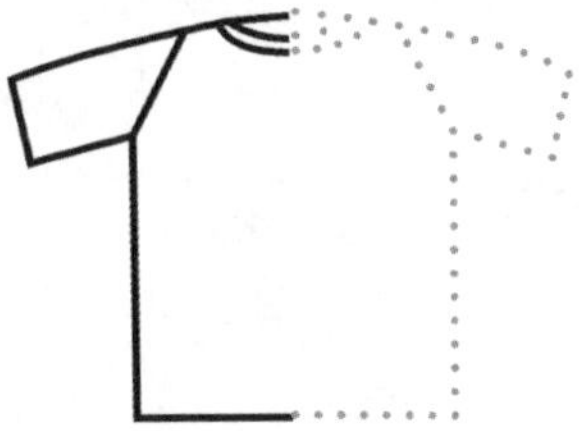

This is my ______.

6

These are my ______.

4 Write.

1

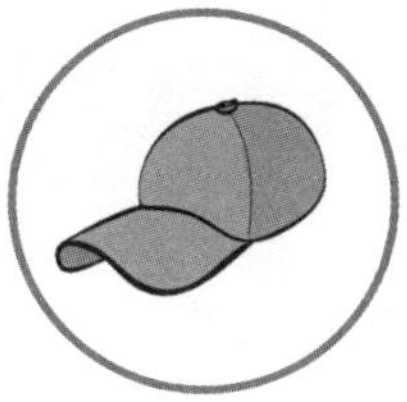

Put on your cap!

2

Put on ______!

3

______

4

______

1 Read and number.

1. his jacket
2. her jacket
3. her socks
4. his socks
5. his T-shirt
6. her T-shirt

a 

b 

c 

d 

e 

f 

2 Read and circle.

1 

This is his / her jacket.

2 

This is his / her hat.

3 

These are his / her trousers.

4 

This is his / her skirt.

5 

These are his / her shoes.

6 

This is his / her cap.

3 Write. **his** **her**

1 This is ___her T-shirt___.

2 This is ________________.

3 These are ________________.

4 These are ________________.

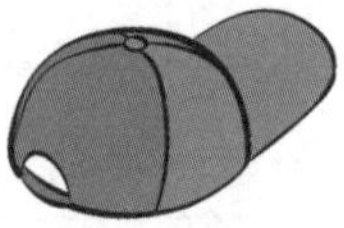

5 This is ________________.

4 Follow and write.

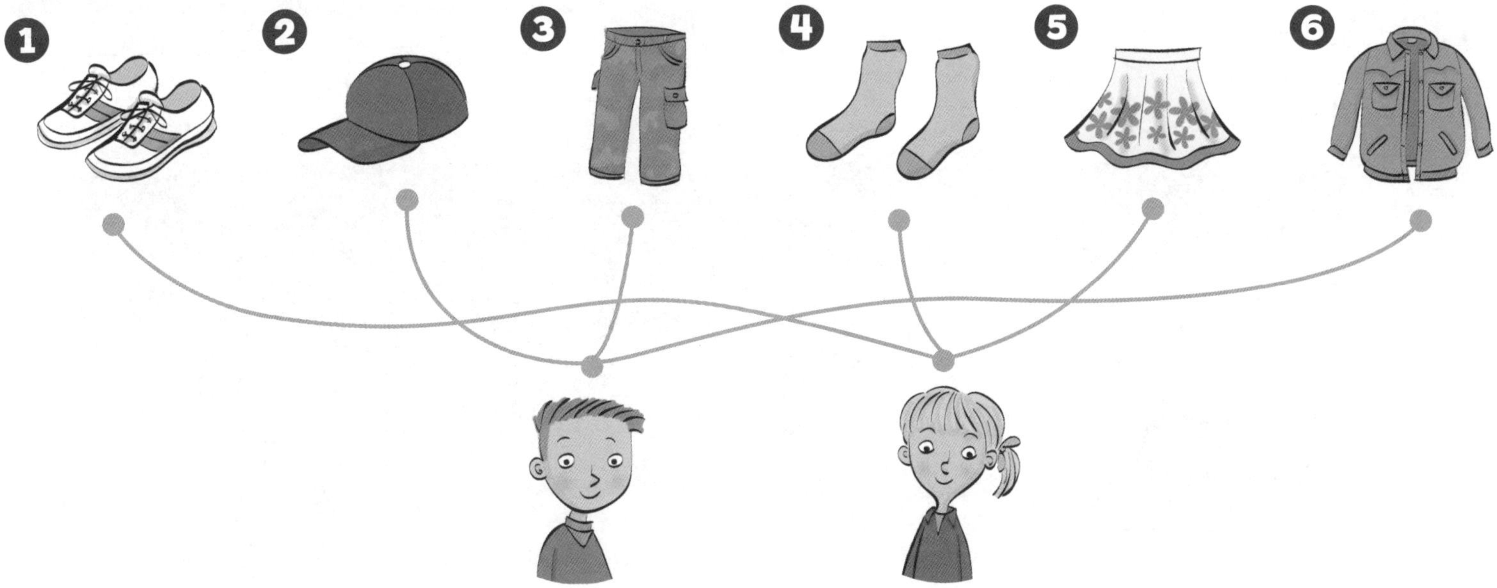

1 ___These are___ her shoes.

2 ________________ his cap.

3 ________________ his trousers.

4 ________________

5 ________________

6 ________________

➜ Go to Grammar check page 130

1 Find, circle and write.

1 

new

2 

c

3 

l

p	l	o	a	q	b	u	b	o
n	t	b	s	d	m	n	e	w
e	r	f	h	o	t	g	a	h
c	o	l	o	u	r	f	u	l
m	l	i	r	u	i	n	t	u
b	d	s	t	u	o	r	i	i
v	c	h	a	l	e	s	f	r
a	e	k	l	o	n	g	u	p
o	l	i	n	k	r	o	l	o

4 

b

5 

s

6 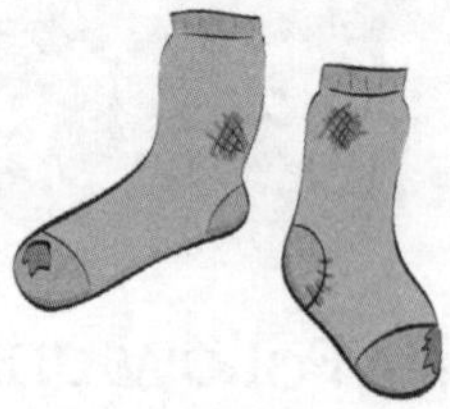

o

2 Read and write the letters.

1 Her hat is old. d

2 His shoes are old. ____

3 His socks are long. ____

4 His jacket is new. ____

5 Her jacket is colourful. ____

6 Her hat is new. ____

7 His trousers are short. ____

8 Her skirt is beautiful. ____

3 Read and tick ✔.

1

a Those shoes are beautiful. ☑
b That shoe is beautiful. ☐

2

a Those jackets are colourful. ☐
b That jacket is colourful. ☐

3

a That sock is long. ☐
b Those socks are long. ☐

4

a That cap is old. ☐
b Those caps are old. ☐

5

a That hat is new. ☐
b Those hats are new. ☐

4 Write. **That Those** **is are**

1

2

3

4

5

6

1 Those trousers are new.
2 ____________ skirts ____________ old.
3 ____________ cap ____________ colourful.
4 ____________ socks ____________ beautiful.
5 ____________ shoes ____________ long.
6 ____________ jacket ____________ short.

➜ Go to Grammar check page 130

1 Look at the pictures. What clothes can you see?

2 Read the story.

Rabbit and Duck

3 Read again and match.

1  Her cap is old.

2  I've got a jacket and a hat.

3  This hat is beautiful.

4  These socks are long.

a 

b 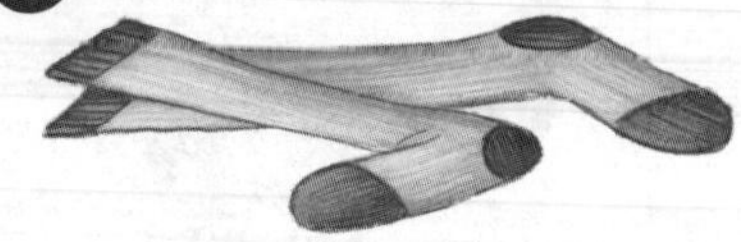

c 

d 

4 Write.

catch ~~cold~~ can Yes

1  Are you cold?  ______, I am.

2  Can you ______?  Yes, I ______.

5 Circle, tick ✔ and colour.

1 **Circle.**
My favourite part of the story is

1 2 3
4 5 6

2 **Tick ✔.**
My favourite character is

 ☐  ☐

3 **Colour.**
How many stars for the story?

☆ ☆ ☆ ☆ ☆

Reading

1 Find and circle. Then write.

dressfeathersshirtmask

❶ 
dress

❷ 
______

❸ 
______

❹ 
______

2 Read and colour.

Home
About me
Links

Latest posts
10 February
12 March

Search

Clothes in my country: Carnival

I'm Lara. I'm from Italy.

These are my Carnival clothes.

I've got a dress and a big hat. My dress is colourful. It's green, yellow and blue. My hat is pink and blue. These shoes are new and red.

This is my brother. He's got trousers and a jacket. His trousers are yellow. His jacket is new. It's red, yellow and blue. His mask is black.

Comments:

Writing

3 Circle the plural endings. Then write. **is** **are**

1 Those shoes are brown.

2 That shirt ________ new.

3 These socks ________ long.

4 This dress ________ colourful.

4 Think about a family member. Write your ideas.

Favourite clothes

Family member	Clothes	Adjective
________	T-shirt	colourful
	________	________
	________	________

5 Choose a family member. Read. Then write for you and draw.

This is my brother.
This is his T-shirt. It's new.
These are his trousers.
They're long.
These are his shoes.
They're colourful.

This is my ________

____

____

____

____

____

____

7 Review

1 Look, read and number.

a trousers [ ]

b skirt [ ]

c jacket [1]

d cap [ ]

e T-shirt [ ]

f shoes [ ]

2 Look at 1 and write.

his **her**

1

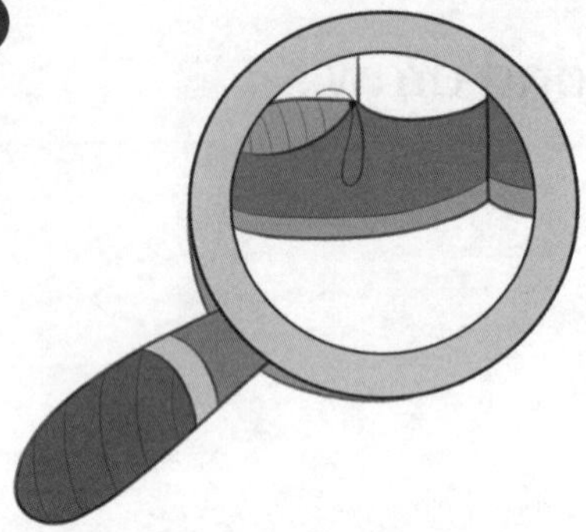

These are his shoes.

2

This is ______ ______.

3

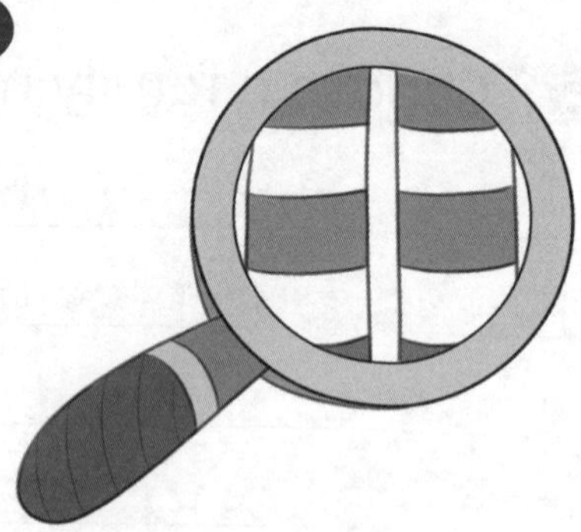

______

______

4

______

______

5

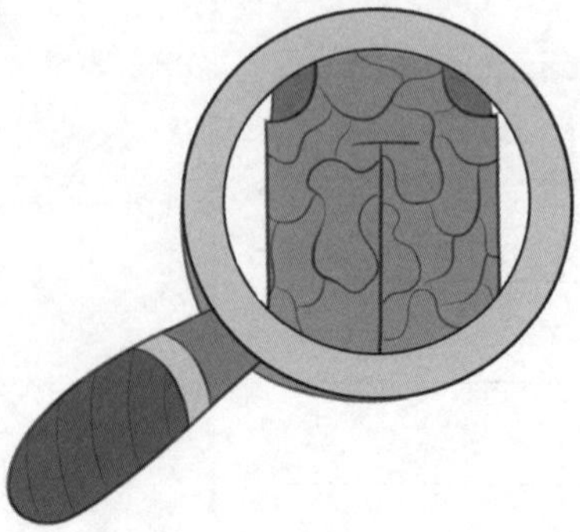

______

______

6

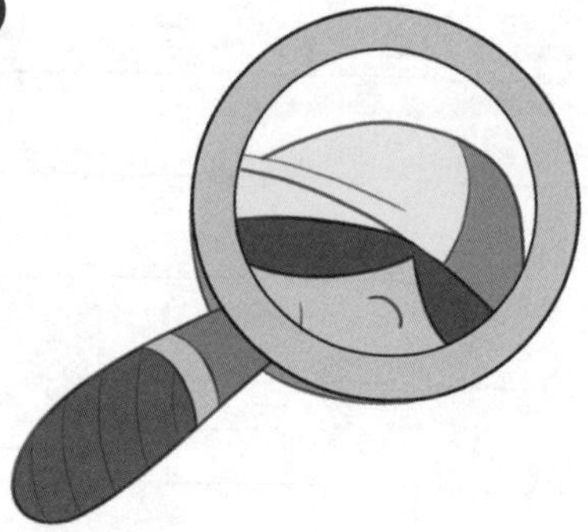

______

______

7

3 Circle the odd one out.

1 T-shirt new shoes
2 dress skirt beautiful
3 long short shirt
4 colourful old jacket
5 long cap socks
6 beautiful colourful feathers

4 Write.

1 jacket That new. is

That jacket is new.

2 old. are Those feathers

3 hat That beautiful. is

4 are socks short. Those

5 shirt is That colourful.

Unit 7 My progress ✓

I can talk about clothes.	✓	✓	✓
I can use *This is his/her* and *These are his/her.*	✓	✓	✓
I can use adjectives to describe clothes.	✓	✓	✓
I can read a story.	✓	✓	✓
I can write about clothes.	✓	✓	✓
I can make a paper chain of girls and boys.	✓	✓	✓

My effort

Excellent!

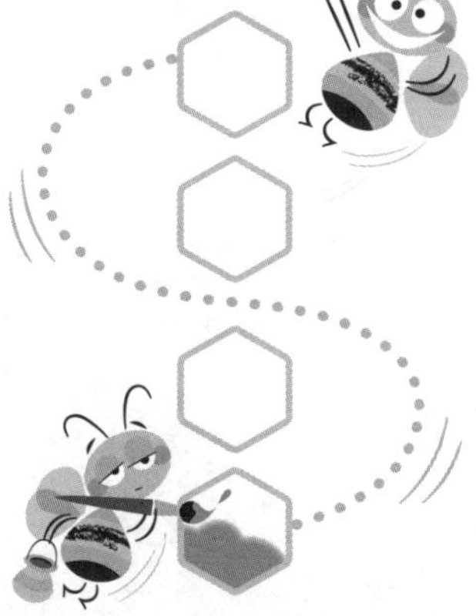

8 Food
Lesson 1 Words

1 Read and number.

1 kiwis
2 apples
3 strawberries
4 oranges
5 grapes
6 bananas
7 pears
8 mangoes

2 Write.

1  oranges

2 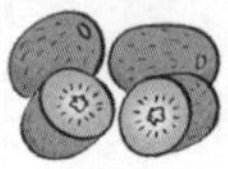 ____________

3 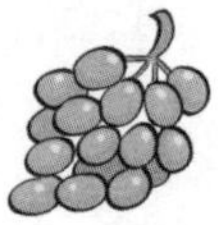 ____________

4  ____________

5  ____________

6  ____________

7  ____________

8  ____________

3 Read and colour.

1 = red	2 = green	3 = purple	4 = orange	5 = yellow

4 Look at 3 and write.

1 The kiwis are green.
2 The ______ are orange.
3 The ______ are purple.
4 The ______ are red.
5 The ______ are yellow.
6 The ______ are green.

5 Read, count and write.

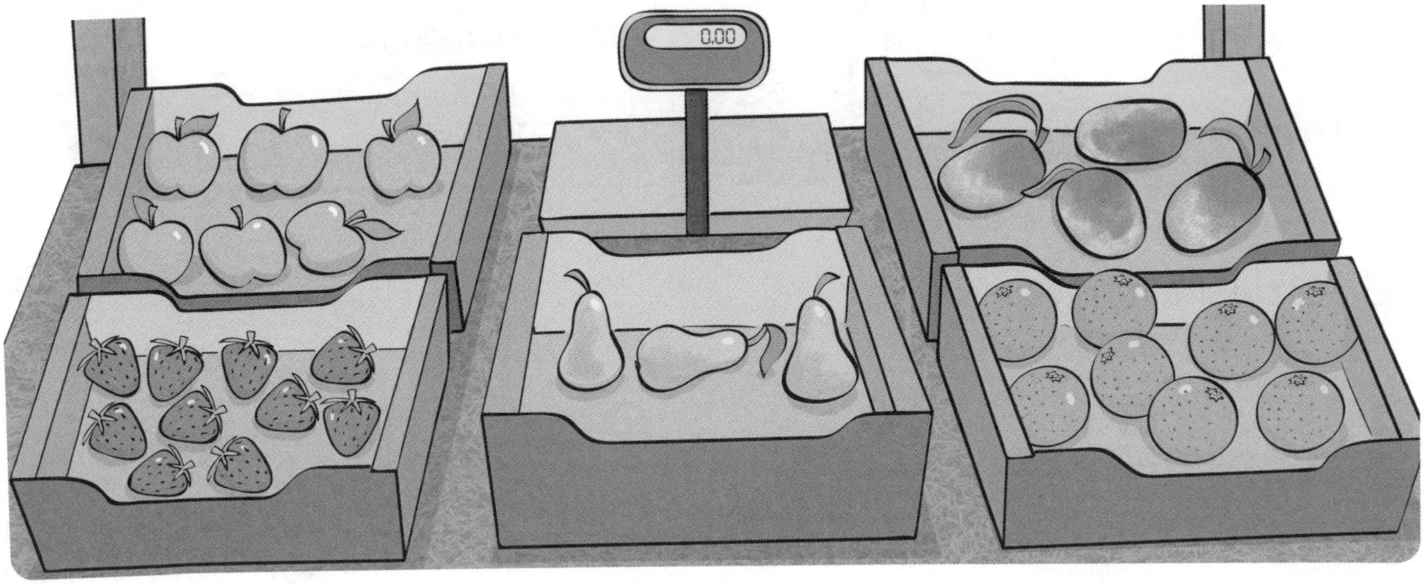

1 How many apples? Six apples.
2 How many oranges? ______
3 How many strawberries? ______
4 How many mangoes? ______
5 How many pears? ______

1 Read and tick ✔.

1

I like strawberries.	☐
I like grapes.	✔

2

I don't like apples.	☐
I don't like pears.	☐

3

I like oranges.	☐
I don't like oranges.	☐

4

I don't like mangoes.	☐
I like mangoes.	☐

2 Circle the fruit you like.

1 

2 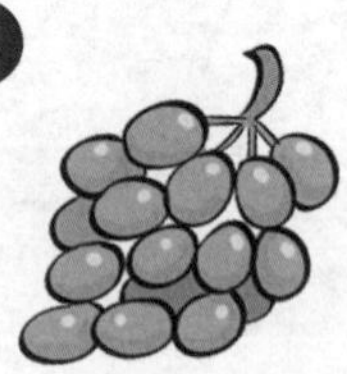

3 

4 

5 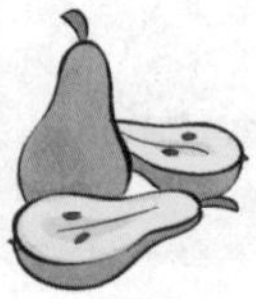

6 

3 Look at **2** and write. **like** **don't like**

1 I ____________________ kiwis.

2 I ____________________ grapes.

3 I ____________________ oranges.

4 I ____________________ bananas.

5 I ____________________ pears.

6 I ____________________ mangoes.

4 Read and write the names.

1

I like apples.
I like oranges.
I don't like mangoes.
I like grapes.
My name is ______________.

2

I like oranges.
I like apples.
I don't like mangoes.
I don't like strawberries.
My name is ______________.

5 Write.

1 I like strawberries.
2 ______________
3 ______________
4 I don't like ______________.
5 ______________
6 ______________

Go to Grammar check page 131

1 Find and circle. Write.

icecreamnoodlessoupsaladjuice(pizza)

❶

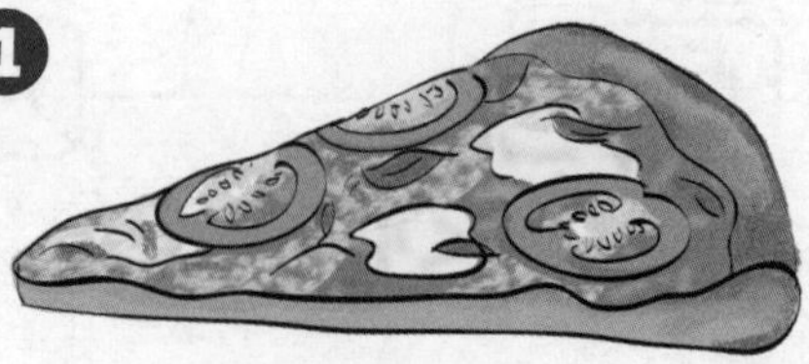

pizza

❷

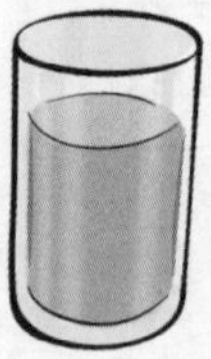

____

❸

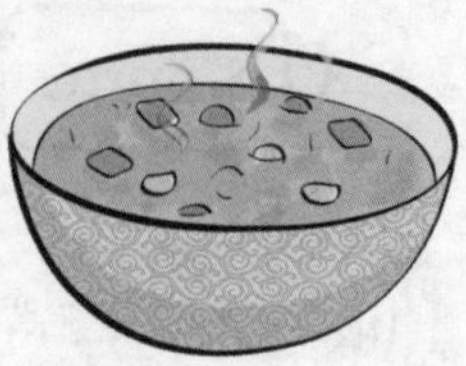

____

❹

____

❺

____

❻

____

2 What do you like? Write. **like** **don't like**

1  I __________ noodles.

2 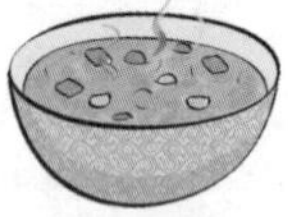 __________

3  __________

4  __________

5  __________

6  __________

3 Read and number.

1 Can I have some noodles, please?
2 Can I have some salad, please?
3 Can I have some soup, please?
4 Can I have some ice cream, please?
5 Can I have some juice, please?
6 Can I have some pizza, please?

a
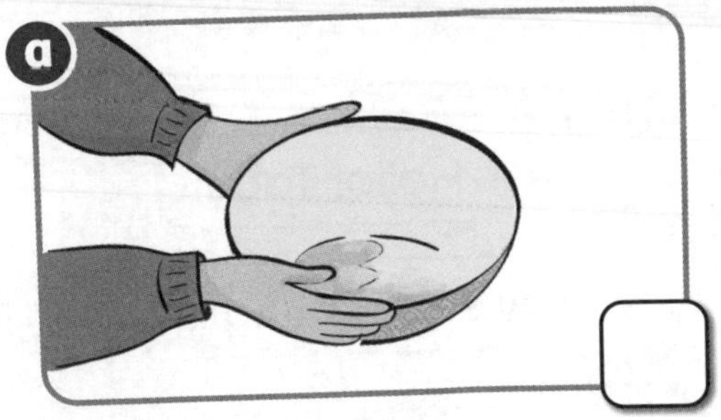

b
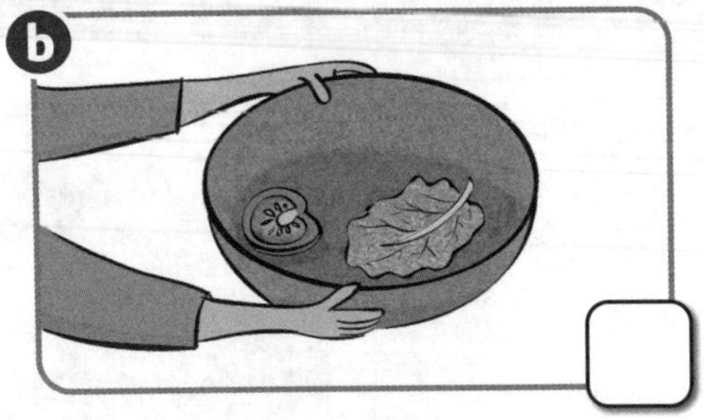

c
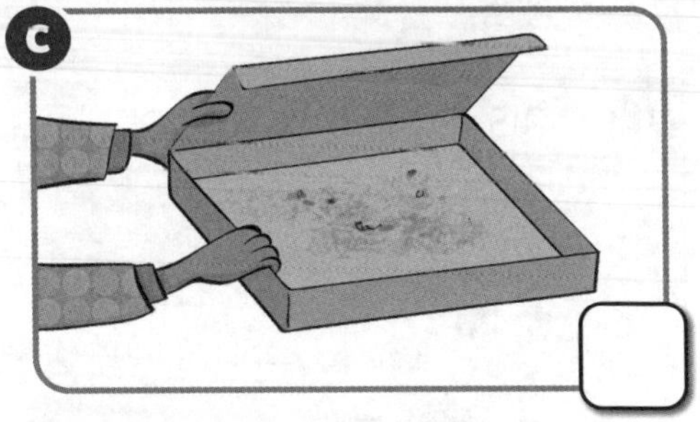

d

1

e

f

4 Write the questions and answers.

1 Can I have some salad, please?
2 Yes, ______________________________.
3 Can ______________________________?
4 ______________________________
5 ______________________________
6 ______________________________

➜ Go to Grammar check page 131

1 Look at the pictures. Which food can you see?

2 Read the story.

Noodles for Toby

3 Read again and write *T* (true) or *F* (false).

1 Toby is hungry. T
2 Shen's dad has got some salad. ___
3 Shen's dad has got some soup. ___
4 Toby likes soup. ___
5 Shen can eat his noodles. ___
6 Toby likes noodles. ___

4 Order the words.

1 hungry? Are you

Are ______________________________

2 noodles. I've some got

____

3 eat I my noodles. can't

____

5 Circle, tick ✔ and colour.

1 **Circle.**
My favourite part of the story is

1 2 3
4 5 6

2 **Tick ✔.**
My favourite character is

3 **Colour.**
How many stars for the story?

Reading

1 Write. **eggs** **cheese** **~~bread~~** **olives**

1 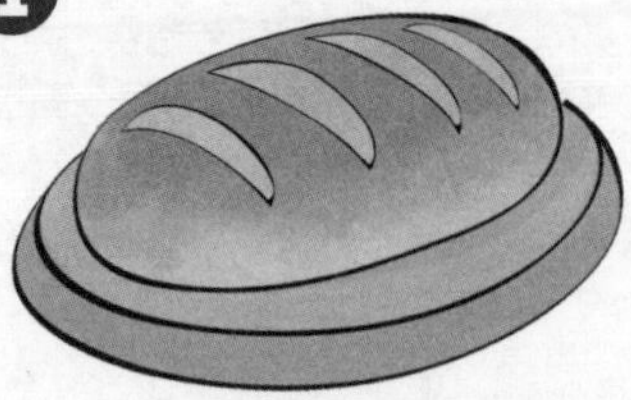
2 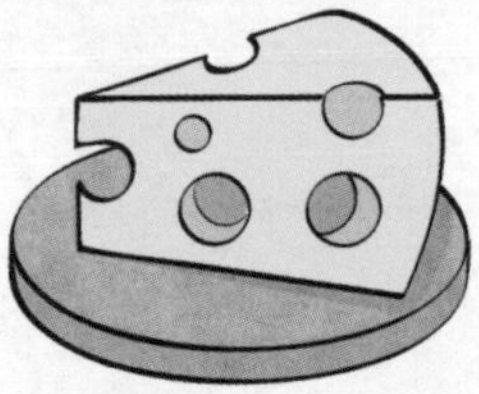
3 
4 

1 bread ________ 2 ________ 3 ________ 4 ________

2 Read and number.

1 

I don't like soup for breakfast.
I like bread.

My favourite breakfast is bread, fish and eggs.

I like orange juice, too.

2 

I don't like fish for breakfast.
I like fruit.

My favourite breakfast is eggs and bread.

I like mango juice, too.

3 

I don't like bread for breakfast.
I like soup.

My favourite breakfast is soup and fish.

I like salad, too.

a  ☐

b  ☐

c  ☐

Writing

3 Rewrite the sentences with *n't*.

1 I do not like bread. I don't like bread.

2 No, I do not. ______

3 I do not like fish. ______

4 I do not. ______

4 Write your ideas.

Breakfast in my country

Like ☺	Don't like ☹	My favourite ☆☆☆

5 Read. Then write for you and draw.

I like soup for breakfast.
I don't like fish.
My favourite breakfast
is bread and cheese.
I like bananas, too.

I like ______

1 Match and write.

1 ki — berries — 

2 ban — cream — 

3 man — wis — 

4 straw — goes — 

5 ice — anas — 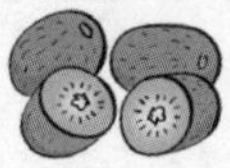 kiwis

2 Colour the fruit words green.

grapes	noodles	apples	oranges
eggs	olives	mangoes	pears

3 Read and draw.

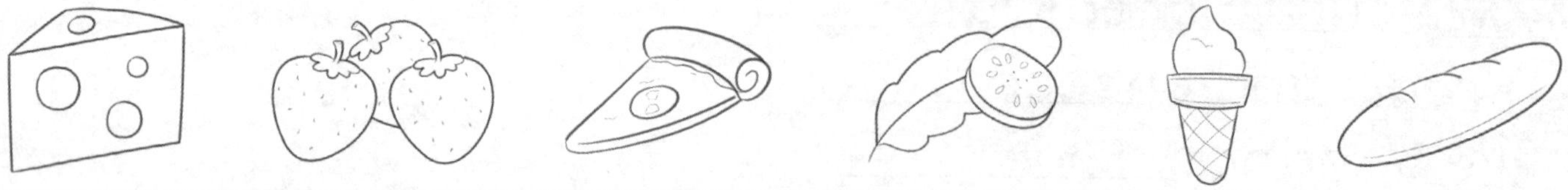

I don't like cheese and
I don't like bread.
I like salad and I like pizza.
I don't like ice cream.
I like strawberries!

4 Order the words.

1 like olives. I — I like olives.

2 like soup. don't I — ______

3 juice? like you Do — ______

4 don't. I No, — ______

5 Write questions.

eggs **ice cream** ~~**cheese**~~ **bread**

1 Can I have some cheese, please?

2 ______

3 ______

4 ______

Unit 8 My progress ✔

I can talk about fruit.	✔	✔	✔
I can use *I like* and *I don't like*.	✔	✔	✔
I can read a story.	✔	✔	✔
I can ask for food.	✔	✔	✔
I can write about my breakfast.	✔	✔	✔
I can do a shopping role play.	✔	✔	✔

My effort

Excellent!

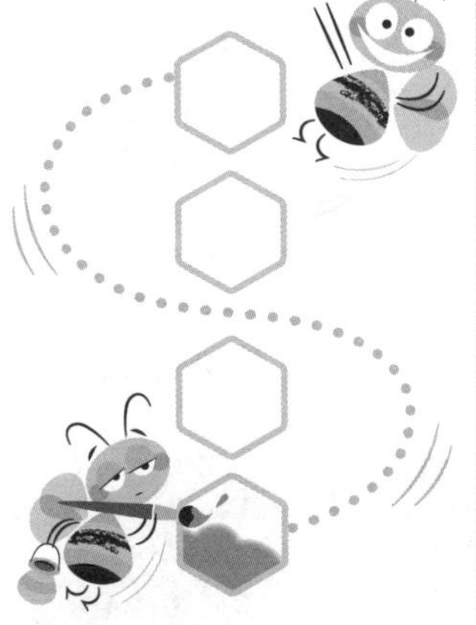

9 At home
Lesson 1 Words

1 Read and number.

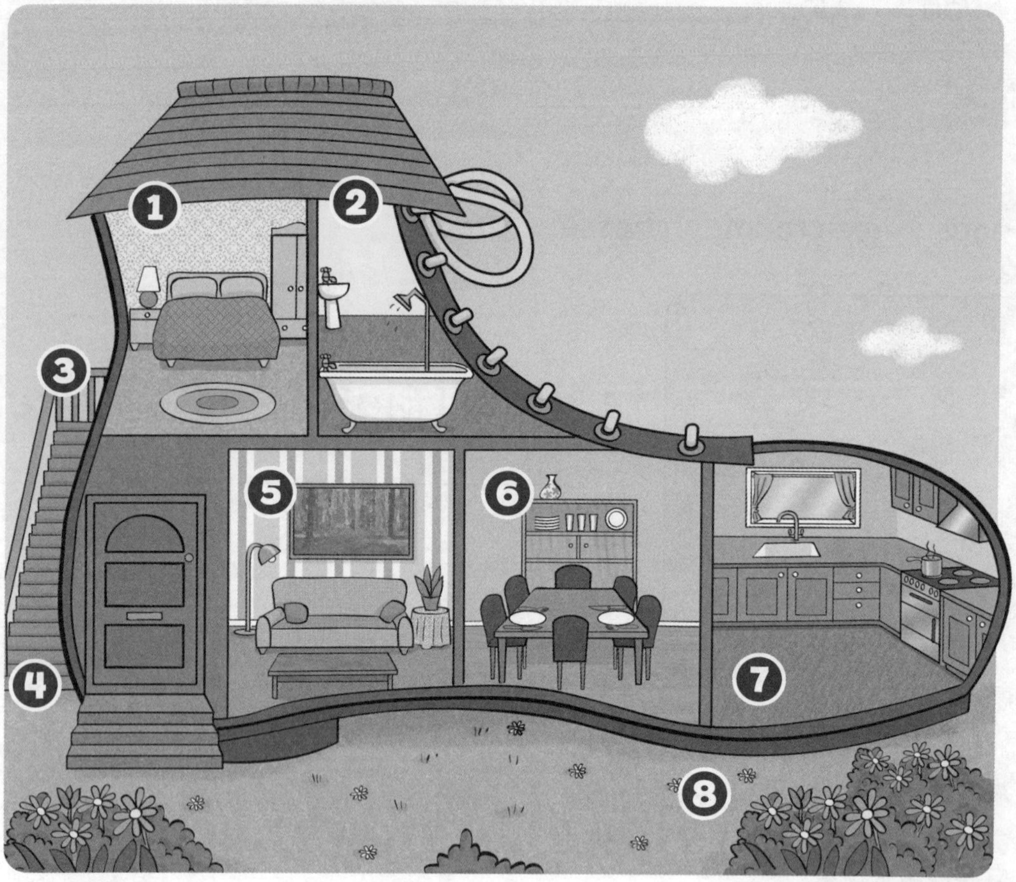

bedroom	1
living room	
bathroom	
kitchen	
dining room	
garden	
downstairs	
upstairs	

2 Write.

1 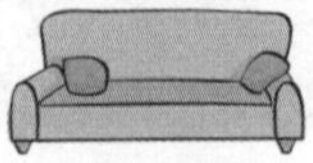 living room

2  ______

3  ______

4  ______

5  ______

6  ______

7  ______

8  ______

3 Write.

1 He's in the bedroom.
2 She's in the ______.
3 She's in the ______.
4 He's in the ______.
5 She's in the ______.
6 He's in the ______.

1

2

3

4

5

6

4 Write. **upstairs** **downstairs**

1 Where's the bathroom?
It's upstairs.
2 Where's the dining room?
It's ______.
3 Where's the living room?
It's ______.
4 Where's the bedroom?
It's ______.
5 Where's kitchen?
It's ______.
6 Where's the boy?
He's ______.

1 Read and match.

1 Is Grandma in the bathroom?

2 Is Hugo in the dining room?

3 Is Dad in the living room?

4 Is Mum in the bedroom?

Yes, he is.

Yes, she is.

No, she isn't.

No, he isn't.

2 Read and circle.

1 Is SuperT upstairs? Yes, he is. / Yes, she is.

2 Is SuperK downstairs? Yes, he is. / No, he isn't.

3 Is SuperS in the dining room? Yes, he is. / No, he isn't.

4 Is SuperJ in the dining room? Yes, she is. / No, she isn't.

5 Is SuperF in the bathroom? No, she isn't. / No, he isn't.

6 Is SuperL in the garden? Yes, she is. / No, she isn't.

3 Write. **Yes, he is.** **Yes, she is.** **No, he isn't.** ~~**No, she isn't.**~~

1 

Is Emma in the dining room?

No, she isn't.

2 

Is Adam in the bathroom?

____

3 

Is Mum in the living room?

____

4 

Is Peter upstairs?

____

4 Order the words. Then tick ✔ or cross ✘.

1 

he | Is | the | in | kitchen?

Is he in the kitchen? ✔

2 

the | bedroom? | he | Is | in

______________________ ☐

3 

she | Is | garden? | in | the

______________________ ☐

4 

downstairs? | he | Is

______________________ ☐

5 

Is | she | bathroom? | the | in

______________________ ☐

➔ Go to Grammar check page 132

1 Order the letters. Write.

1
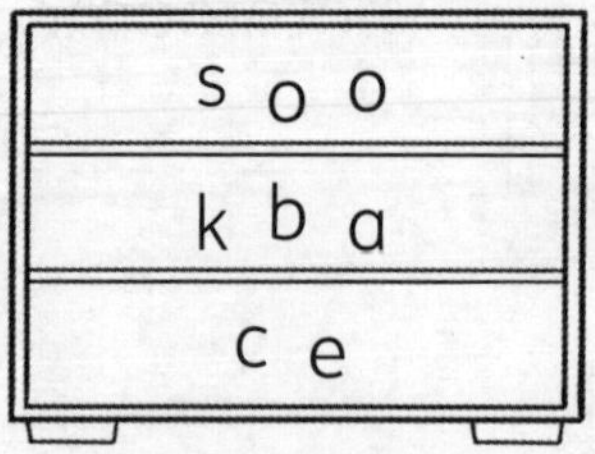

bookcase

2
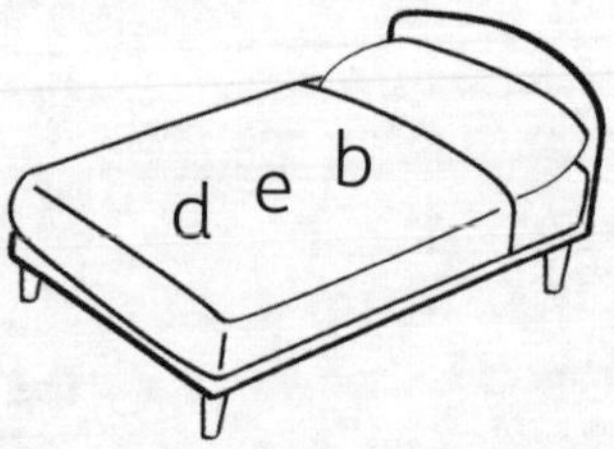

____

3
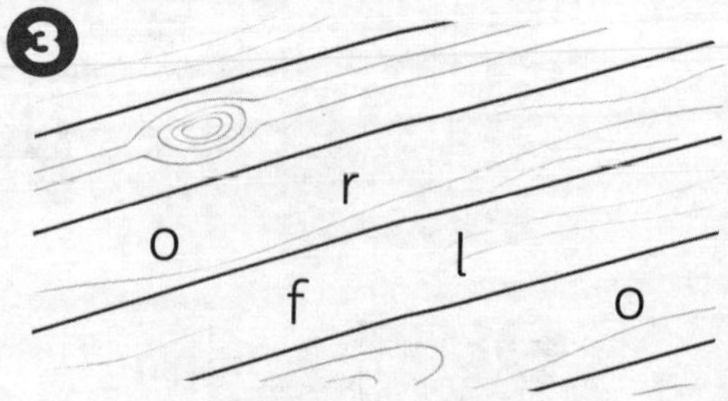

____

4
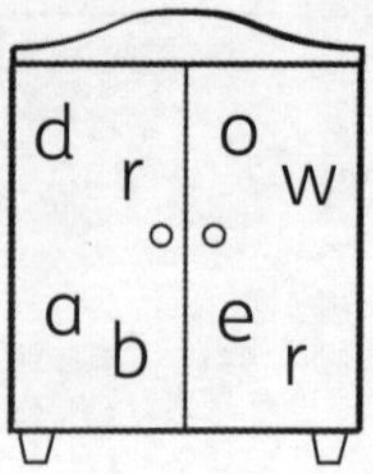

____

5
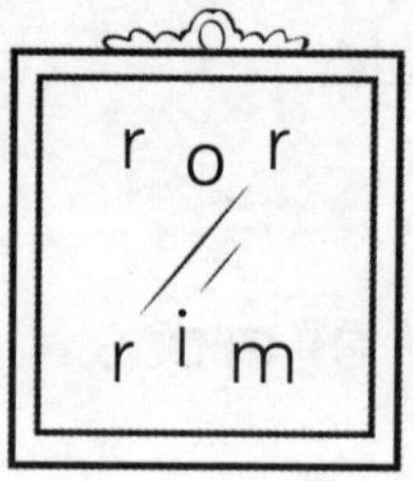

____

6
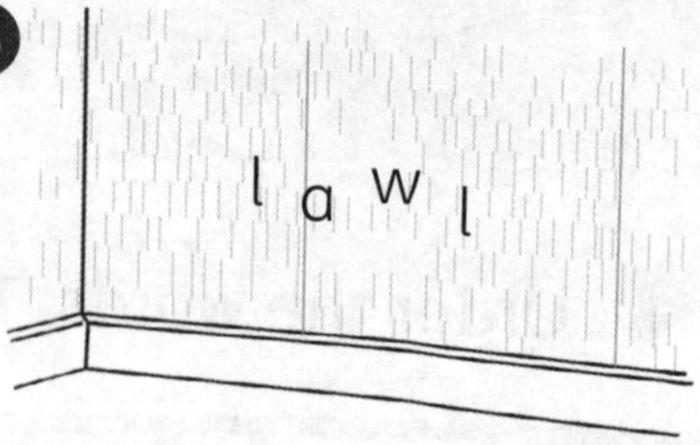

____

2 Read, draw and colour.

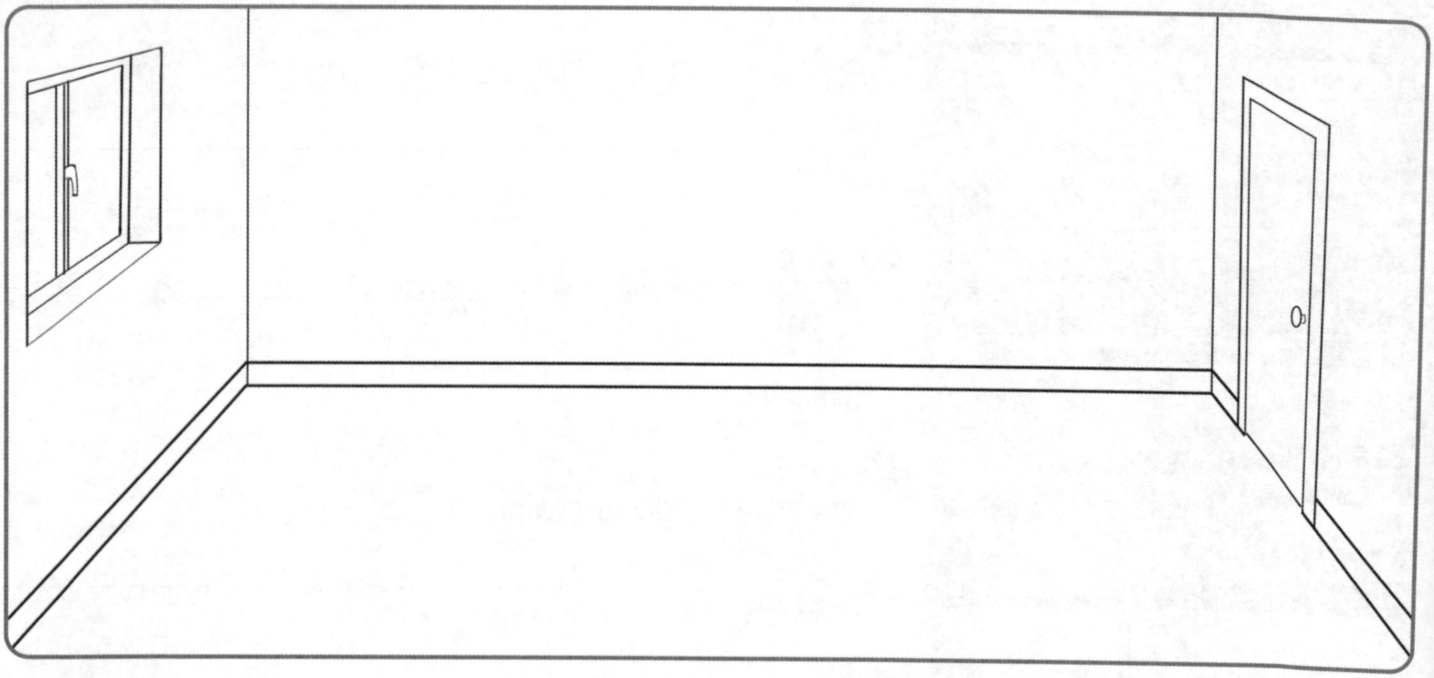

1 There's a bed.

2 There's a wardrobe.

3 There's a bookcase.

4 There's a mirror.

5 The wall is blue.

6 The floor is brown.

3 Write and circle.

1 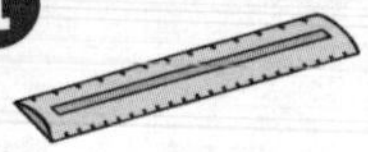 Where's my ruler? ______ It's (on) / **under** the bookcase.

2  ______ It's **on / in** the chair.

3  ______ It's **under / in** the bed.

4  ______ It's **on / in** the wardrobe.

4 Look at 3 and write.

in **on** **under**

1 Where's my ball?  It's under the mirror.

2 Where's my teddy?  ______

3 Where's my bag?  ______

4 Where's my jacket?  ______

➜ Go to Grammar check page 132

1 Look at the pictures. Where's the tortoise?

2 Read the story.

Where's my tortoise?

3 Read again and circle *True* or *False*.

1 The tortoise is in the kitchen. True / False
2 The cap is in the bookcase. True / False
3 The bag is under the chair. True / False
4 The tortoise is in the living room. True / False
5 The tortoise is under the tree. True / False
6 Mia is happy. True / False

4 Write. **bookcase** ~~**in**~~ **garden** **under**

1 It isn't ___in___ the kitchen.

2 It's in the __________!

3 Is it __________ the chair?

4 Is it in the __________?

5 Circle, tick ✔ and colour.

1 **Circle.**
My favourite part of the story is

1 2 3

4 5 6

2 **Tick ✔.**
My favourite character is

3 **Colour.**
How many stars for the story?

Reading

1 Write. **sofa** **cushions** **table** ~~**picture**~~

1 picture

2 ______

3 ______

4 ______

2 Read and circle *True* or *False*.

Dear Diary,
I'm in my new home! There are two bedrooms and two bathrooms. There's a kitchen and a living room. I like my bedroom. There's a bed, a chair and a desk. There are pictures on the wall. My teddy is on the floor. This is the living room. There's a sofa and cushions. There's a mirror on the wall.
Julia

1 There are three bedrooms. True / (False)
2 There isn't a kitchen. True / False
3 There's a desk in the bedroom. True / False
4 The teddy is on the bed. True / False
5 The mirror is on the wall. True / False

Writing

3 Write full stops **.** or questions marks **?** .

1 Is my dad in the living room ___?___
2 There are two bathrooms ______
3 This is my bedroom ______
4 Where's the mirror ______

4 Circle the places and furniture in your home.

bathroom   bedroom   dining room   garden   kitchen   living room
bed   bookcase   cushions   mirror   picture   sofa   table   wardrobe

5 Read. Then write for you and draw.

This is my house.
There's a kitchen and
a living room. There are
three bedrooms and
a bathroom.
Dad is in the garden.
My cat is under the tree.

This is ______________________
____
____
____
____
____
____
____

1 Write. Then match.

a	b	c	d	e	f	g	h	i	j	k	l	m
Δ	*	°	+	√	∞	↓	~	→	•	Ω	&	£
n	**o**	**p**	**q**	**r**	**s**	**t**	**u**	**v**	**w**	**x**	**y**	**z**
$	@	!	#	<	}	=	%	➤	?	\	Ö	Ø

1 * Δ = ~ < @ @ £
bathroom

2 + → $ → $ ↓ < @ @ £
____

3 % ! } = Δ → < }
____

4 + @ ? $ } = Δ → < }
____

5 ↓ Δ < + √ $
____

6 & → ➤ → $ ↓ < @ @ £
____

a

b

c

d

e

f

2 Read and draw.

1 Where's the plane?
It's in the bookcase.

2 Where's the cushion?
It's on the sofa.

3 Where's the cap?
It's under the table.

4 Where's the ball?
It's on the floor.

3 Write the questions and answers.

1 ■s Ryan ■own■tairs? Is Ryan downstairs?
■es, he ■s. Yes, ______.

2 Is Grandma i■ the b■dr■■m? ______
N■, she ■■n't. ______

3 I■ she ■n the ■itc■en? ______
Y■s, sh■ is. ______

4 Where's the spider? Write.

in	on	under

1

It's ___on___ the mirror.

2

It's ______ the bed.

3

It's ______ the wardrobe.

4

It's ______ the wall.

Unit 9 My progress ✓

I can talk about places at home. ✓ ✓ ✓
I can ask and answer *Is he / she in the … ?* ✓ ✓ ✓
I can describe where something is. ✓ ✓ ✓
I can read a story. ✓ ✓ ✓
I can write about my home. ✓ ✓ ✓
I can make a model room. ✓ ✓ ✓

My effort

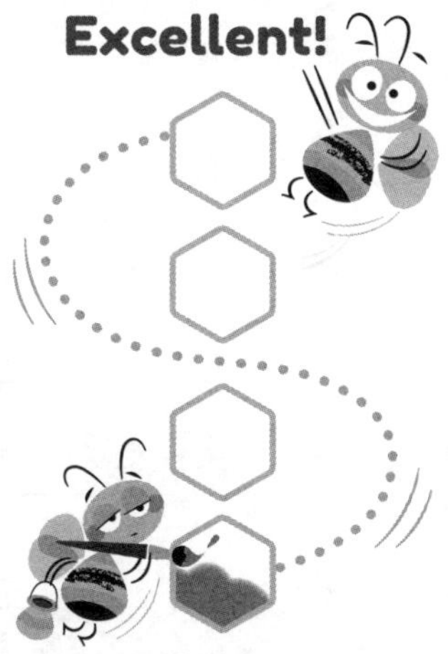

10 At the farm
Lesson 1 Words

1 Read and circle.

❶

horse
donkey

❷

bird
mouse

❸

sheep
cow

❹

goat
chicken

❺

mouse
sheep

❻

cow
horse

❼

sheep
goat

❽

donkey
cow

2 Write.

1 bird
2 ____________
3 ____________
4 ____________
5 ____________
6 ____________
7 ____________
8 ____________

3 Write the animal. Then write *two* or *four*.

1 It's a sheep.
It's got four legs.

2 It's a ______.
It's got ______ legs.

3 It's a ______.
It's got ______ legs.

4 It's a ______.
It's got ______ legs.

5 It's a ______.
It's got ______ legs.

4 Read and write the letter. Then write. **Yes, I do.** **No, I don't.**

a

b

c

1 Do you like goats?
Yes, I do. [b]

2 Do you like cows?
______ [ ]

3 Do you like horses?
______ [ ]

4 Do you like sheep?
______ [ ]

5 Do you like birds?
______ [ ]

6 Do you like donkeys?
______ [ ]

d

e

f

10 Lesson 2 Grammar

1 Read and circle.

1 Are they birds? (Yes, they are.) / No, they aren't.

2 Are they donkeys? Yes, they are. / No, they aren't.

3 Are they mice? Yes, they are. / No, they aren't.

4 Are they cows? Yes, they are. / No, they aren't.

5 Are they horses? Yes, they are. / No, they aren't.

6 Are they chickens? Yes, they are. / No, they aren't.

2 Write. **Are they** **they are** **they aren't**

3 Order the letters. Write the questions. Then tick ✔ or cross ✗.

1 togas Are they goats?  ✗

2 peshe ______  ☐

3 shores ______  ☐

4 cime ______  ☐

5 wocs ______  ☐

6 ckenchis ______  ☐

4 Follow and write.

Yes, they are. **No, they aren't.**

1 

2 

3 

4 

5 

6 

Are they donkeys? ______

Are they sheep? No, they aren't.

Are they birds? ______

Are they cows? ______

Are they goats? ______

Are they horses? ______

➜ Go to Grammar check page 133

1 Read and tick ✔.

1 

- clean ☐
- dirty ✔

2 

- clean ☐
- noisy ☐

3 

- big ☐
- small ☐

4 

- big ☐
- dirty ☐

5 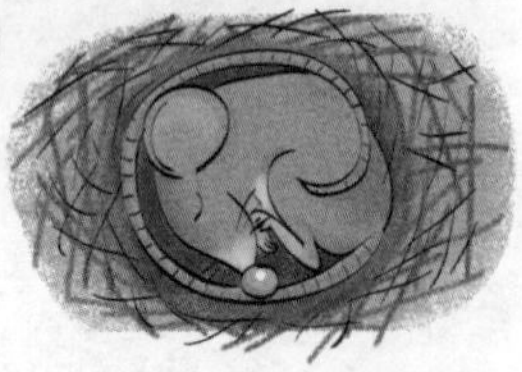

- quiet ☐
- noisy ☐

6 

- small ☐
- noisy ☐

2 Write.

1  It's big.

2  ______________

3  ______________

4  ______________

5  ______________

6  ______________

3 Read and number.

1 It's a small donkey.
2 It's a dirty goat.
3 They're noisy cows.
4 It's a clean goat.
5 They're quiet cows.
6 They're big donkeys.

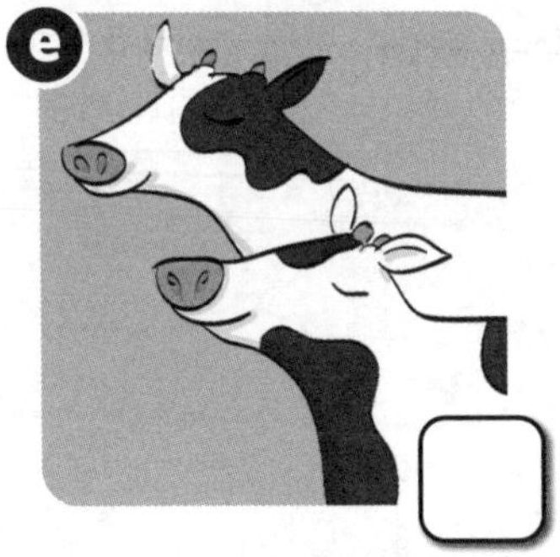

4 Write.

~~clean~~	quiet	dirty
mice	fish	~~ducks~~

big	small	noisy
frog	snake	bee

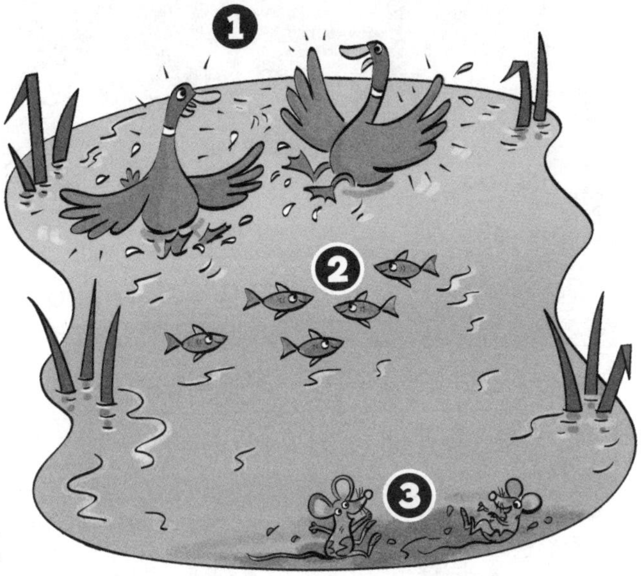

1 They're clean ducks.
2 ______________________
3 ______________________
4 It's a ______________________.
5 ______________________
6 ______________________

➜ Go to Grammar check page 133

1 Look at the pictures. What animals can you see?

2 Read the story.

I'm me!

3 Read again and write.

big **clean** ~~**new**~~ **noisy**

1 

She's a ___new___ student.

2 

Look at her hands. They're ____________.

3 

Lalo and Bruno are ____________ students.

4 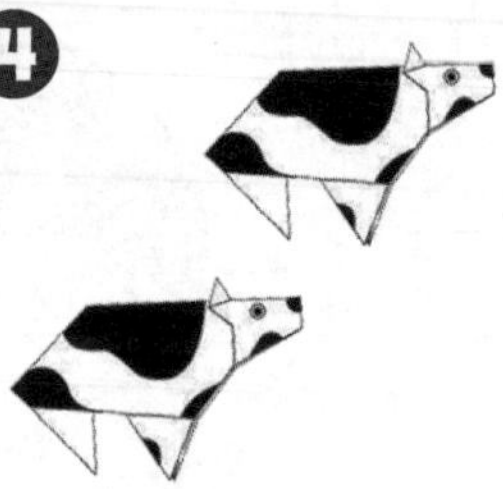

They're ____________ cows.

4 Read and match.

1  Who's she?

2  Are they sheep?

3  I'm small and I'm quiet.

a  No, they're not. They're cows.

b  But I'm me!

c  It's Ana. She's a new student.

5 Circle, tick ✔ and colour.

1 **Circle.**
My favourite part of the story is

1 2 3

4 5 6

2 **Tick ✔.**
My favourite character is

3 **Colour.**
How many stars for the story?

Reading

1 Write. **lemons** ~~**peaches**~~ **pineapples** **watermelons**

1 peaches

2 ______

3 ______

4 ______

2 Read and number.

My farm

4th October

My name's Juan. This is my farm.

It's in Mexico.

These are the animals on my farm.

There are some goats. They're noisy goats. [3]

There are hungry chickens. [ ]

I've got a big dog. His name is Muffin. [ ]

There are colourful fruit trees with lemons and peaches. [ ]

We've got pineapples, too. They're big. [ ]

This is a red and green watermelon. [ ]

Writing

3 Underline the adjectives. Then circle the nouns.

1 They're noisy goats.
2 There are hungry chickens.
3 I've got a big dog.
4 There are colourful trees.

4 Circle what you can see on a farm in your country.

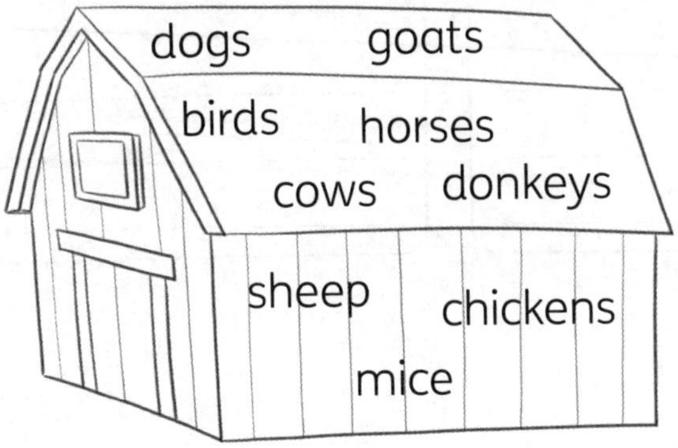

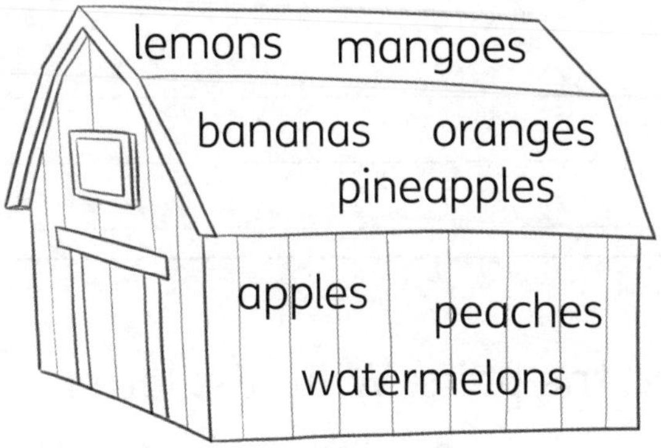

5 Read. Then write for you and draw.

There's a donkey.
It's a noisy donkey.
There are goats and sheep.
They're small sheep.
There are lemon trees.
They're yellow.

There's a __________

10 Review

1 Write the words in the boxes.

bird chicken ~~cow~~ donkey duck goat horse mouse sheep

Animals with tails 

cow

Animals with wings 

2 Find the pairs. Write the letter.

1 big c 2 dirty ___ 3 noisy ___ 4 short ___ 5 new ___ 6 hot ___

a long b old c small d cold e clean f quiet

3 Read and match.

1 Are they watermelons?

2 Are they birds?

3 Are they mice?

Yes, they are.

No, they aren't.

4 Are they pineapples?

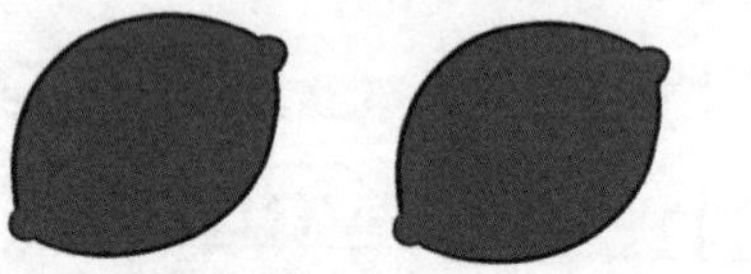

5 Are they sheep?

6 Are they cows?

4 Order the words.

1. It's a goat. clean — It's a clean goat.
2. hungry They're donkeys. — ______
3. dirty a horse. It's — ______
4. lemons. small They're — ______

5 Write.

1. Are they goats?
   No, they aren't.
   They're sheep.
2. Are they cows?
   ______
   ______
3. Are they birds?
   ______
   ______
4. Are they mice?
   ______
   ______

Unit 10 My progress ✓

- I can talk about farm animals.
- I can ask and answer *Are they ... ?*
- I can use adjectives to describe animals.
- I can read a story.
- I can write about a farm.
- I can make a poster about my country.

My effort

Excellent!

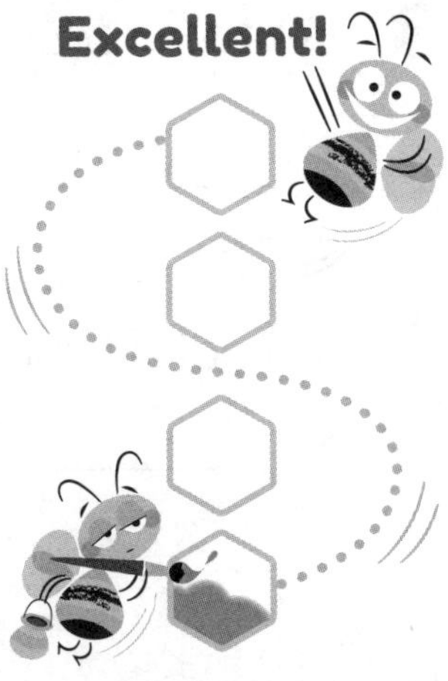

1 Grammar check

What is it? | **It's** a window.

1 Write. **is it** **It's**

1 What is it ? It's a bin.
2 What ____________ ? ____________ a desk.
3 What ____________ ? ____________ a chair.
4 What ____________ ? ____________ a board.

2 Write. **door** **clock** **cupboard**

❶ 

What ____________ ?
It's ____________ .

❷ 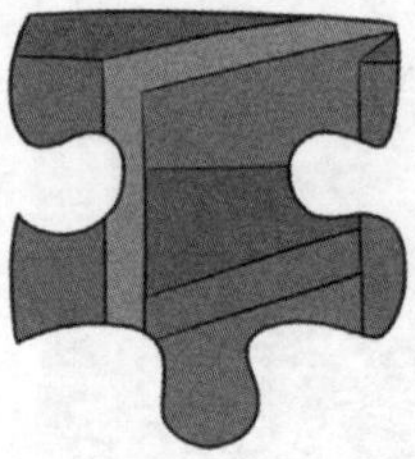

____________ ?
____

❸ 

____________ ?
____

What colour is the door? | **What colour is it?** | **The** door **is** green. | **It's** green.

3 Write. **It's** **clock** ~~**What**~~ **is**

1 What colour is the clock?
2 The ____________ is red.
3 Look at the desk. What colour ____________ it?
4 ____________ green.

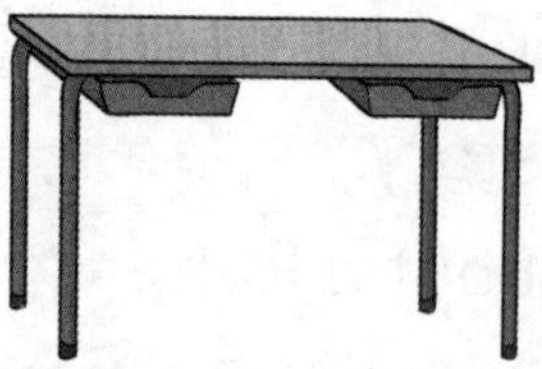

I've got a kite.

I haven't got a plane.

1 Write. **I've got** **I haven't got**

1 ✔ I've got a robot.
2 ✘ ________ a boat.
3 ✔ ________ a board game.
4 ✘ ________ a skipping rope.

2 Order the words.

1 I've kite. a got
I've ________

2 haven't plane. I a got
____

This is my robot.

This is your boat.

3 Write. **my** **your**

1

This is your pencil.

2

This is ________ book.

3

This is ________ bag.

3 Grammar check

I can climb. | **I can't** sing.

1 Write. **can** **can't**

1 ☺ I can play football.

2 ☹ I ______ play basketball.

3 ☹ I ______ play tennis.

4 ☺ I ______ read.

2 Write.

1 sing ✗

I can't sing.

2 draw ✔

______

3 climb ✔

______

4 dance ✗

______

Can you jump? | **Yes, I can. No, I can't.**

3 Read and match. Then write.

1 Can you catch?

2 Can you jump?

3 Can you swim?

4 Can you fly?

a

______

b

______

c

No, I can't.

d

______

Is it a spider?

Yes, it is.
No, it isn't.

1 Write. **it isn't** **Is it** **it is**

1 Is it a bee? Yes, it is.
2 Is it a fish? Yes, ______.
3 Is it a frog? No, ______.
4 ______ a dog? No, it isn't.

2 Write questions and answers.

1 

2 

3 

1 Is it a spider?
______

2 ______ a snake?
______

3 ______ a duck?
______

There's a lake.

There are some trees.

3 Read and circle.

1 There **'s / are** some bees.
2 There **'s / are** a beach.
3 There **'s / are** a frog.
4 There **'s / are** some trees.

4 Write. **There's** **There are some**

1 flower
There's a flower.

2 plants
______
______

3 spider
______

4 shells
______
______

5 Grammar check

This is my face. | **These are** my feet.

1 Read and match.

This is — my nose
These are
my eyes
my body
my hands

2 Write.

1 This is my face.
2 ______
3 ______
4 ______

It's got a tail. | **It's got** four legs.

3 Read and circle.

1 It's got / It's wings. It's / It's got a duck.
2 It's got / It's a cat. It's / It's got a tail.
3 It's / It's got eight legs. It's got / It's a spider.
4 It's / It's got a dog. It's got / It's four legs.

4 Order the words.

1 got It's beak. a
It's ______

2 two got It's ears.
______

Who's he / she? **He's my** brother. **She's my** sister.

1 Write. **He's** **She's**

1 Who's she? She's my mum.
2 Who's he? ______ my uncle.
3 Who's he? ______ my grandpa.
4 Who's she? ______ my aunt.

2 Write.

1 Who's ______? She's my sister.
2 ______? He's my dad.
3 ______? She's my grandma.

Are you cold? **Yes, I am.** **No, I'm not.**

3 Answer for you. **Yes, I am.** **No, I'm not.**

1 Are you happy? ______
2 Are you hot? ______
3 Are you thirsty? ______

4 Write.

1 ______ thirsty?
No, ______.

2 ______ cold?
Yes, ______.

7 Grammar check

This is his / her hat.	**These are his / her** shoes.

1 Read and circle.

1 (sister) This is **his / her** cap.
2 (dad) These are **his / her** trousers.
3 (uncle) These are **his / her** shoes.
4 (aunt) This is **his / her** skirt.

2 Read and tick.

a 

b 

1 These are his ☐ her ☐ socks. 
2 These are his ☐ her ☐ socks. 

That cap **is** old.	**Those** trousers **are** new.

3 Read and circle.

1 **That / Those** T-shirt is colourful.
2 **That / Those** trousers are short.
3 **That / Those** jackets are beautiful.
4 **That / Those** hat is new.

4 Write.

1 Those socks __________ old.
2 That bat __________ long.
3 Those shoes __________ new.

1 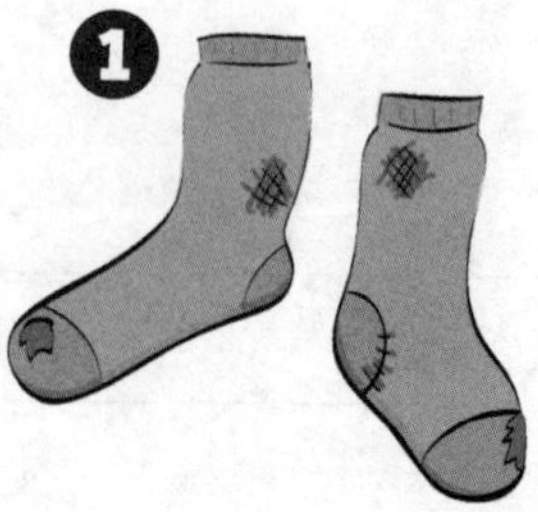

2 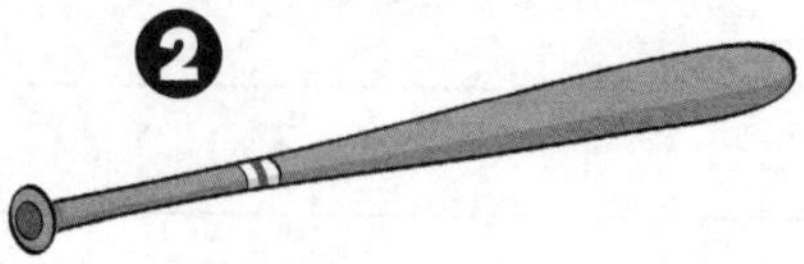

3 

I like strawberries.

I don't like mangoes.

1 Write. like don't like

1 ☹ I don't like bananas.

2 ☺ I ______ mangoes.

3 ☺ I ______ kiwis.

4 ☹ I ______ oranges.

2 Look, read and match.

a I like grapes.

b I don't like grapes.

c I don't like apples.

d I like apples.

Can I have some soup, **please?**

Yes, here you are.
No, sorry!

3 Order the words.

1 please? noodles, I Can some have

Can ______

2 some pizza, Can please? have I

______

4 Read and match.

1 Yes, a sorry!

2 No, b here you are.

9 Grammar check

Is he / she in the bathroom?

Yes, he / she is.
No, he / she isn't.

1 Write.

1 

2 

1 Is he in the dining room? ____________

2 Is she in the living room? ____________

2 Write the questions.

1 Nina is in the bedroom. Is Nina in the bedroom?

2 Dad is in the garden. ____________

3 Mum is downstairs. ____________

Where's the ball?

It's **in / on / under** the chair.

3 Order the words.

1 It's | bed. | the | on — It's ____________

2 wardrobe. | in | the | It's — ____________

3 under | It's | the | table. — ____________

4 Write questions and answers.

1 

Where's the kite?

It's ____________

____

2 

____________ the skipping rope?

____

____

3 

____________ the teddy?

____

____

Are they birds?

Yes, they are.
No, they aren't.

1 Write. **they are** **they aren't**

1 Are they donkeys? Yes, they are.
2 Are they sheep? No, ______.
3 Are they chickens? Yes, ______.
4 Are they mice? No, ______.

2 Write.

1 ______ horses?
2 ______ sheep?
3 ______ goats?
4 ______ birds?

It's a clean goat.

They're dirty chickens.

3 Write. **They're** **It's**

1 They're noisy birds.
2 ______ a small horse.
3 ______ a big dog.
4 ______ quiet cows.

4 Write. **quiet** **noisy**

1

They're ______.

2

______

Wordlist

Unit 1

Lesson 1
bin
board
chair
clock
cupboard
desk
door
window

Lesson 3
black
blue
brown
green
grey
orange
pink
purple
red
white
yellow

Lesson 5
classroom
playground
student
teacher

Unit 2

Lesson 1
ball
board game
boat
kite
plane
robot
skipping rope
teddy

Lesson 3
bag
book
pen
pencil
rubber
ruler

Lesson 5
baseball
bat
scooter
skateboard

Unit 3

Lesson 1
climb
dance
draw
play basketball
play football
play tennis
read
sing

Lesson 3
catch
fly
jump
run
swim
talk

Lesson 5
ice skate
make a snowman
ski
sledge

Unit 4

Lesson 1
bee
cat
dog
duck
fish
frog
snake
spider

Lesson 3
beach
flower
lake
plant
shell
tree

Lesson 5
sand
sandcastle
sea
sun

Unit 5

Lesson 1
arms
body
eyes
face
feet
hands
legs
mouth

Lesson 3
beak
ears
head
nose
tail
wings

Lesson 5
hamster
lizard
rabbit
tortoise

Unit 6

Lesson 1
aunt
brother
dad
grandma
grandpa
mum
sister
uncle

Lesson 3
cold
happy
hot
hungry
sad
thirsty

Lesson 5
baby
boy
cousin
girl

Unit 7

Lesson 1
cap
hat
jacket
shoes
skirt
socks
trousers
T-shirt

Lesson 3
beautiful
colourful
long
new
old
short

Lesson 5
dress
feathers
mask
shirt

Unit 8

Lesson 1
apples
bananas
grapes
kiwis
mangoes
oranges
pears
strawberries

Lesson 3
ice cream
juice
noodles
pizza
salad
soup

Lesson 5
bread
cheese
eggs
olives

Wordlist

Unit 9

Lesson 1
bathroom
bedroom
dining room
downstairs
garden
kitchen
living room
upstairs

Lesson 3
bed
bookcase
floor
mirror
wall
wardrobe

Lesson 5
cushions
picture
sofa
table

Unit 10

Lesson 1
bird
chicken
cow
donkey
goat
horse
mouse
sheep

Lesson 3
big
clean
dirty
noisy
quiet
small

Lesson 5
lemons
peaches
pineapples
watermelons

Test yourself!

1 happy
2 window
3 pen
4 play tennis
5 dog
6 flower
7 sheep
8 grandma
9 bin
10 cap
11 strawberries
12 hands
13 bird
14 mirror